The ...

Book

The Interview Book

Your definitive guide to the perfect interview technique

James Innes

Prentice Hall Business
is an imprint of

Harlow, England • London • New York • Boston • San Francisco • Toronto • Sydney • Singapore • Hong Kong
Tokyo • Seoul • Taipei • New Delhi • Cape Town • Madrid • Mexico City • Amsterdam • Munich • Paris • Milan

PEARSON EDUCATION LIMITED

Edinburgh Gate
Harlow CM20 2JE
Tel: +44 (0)1279 623623
Fax: +44 (0)1279 431059
Website: www.pearsoned.co.uk

First published in Great Britain in 2009

ISBN: 978-0-273-72175-8

British Library Cataloguing-in-Publication Data
A catalogue record for this book is available from the British Library

Library of Congress Cataloging-in-Publication Data

Innes, James
The interview book : your definitive guide to the perfect interview technique / James Innes. -- 1st ed.
p. cm.
Includes bibliographical references and index.
ISBN 978-0-273-72175-8 (pbk. : alk. paper) 1. Employment interviewing. I. Title.
HF5549.5.I6I55 2009
650.14'4--dc22

2009020715

10 9 8 7 6 5
13 12 11

Typeset in 9.5/13pt in Din Regular by 30
Printed in Great Britain by Henry Ling Limited, at the Dorset Press, Dorchester, DT1 1HD

This book is dedicated to my brother, Christian – for showing me the meaning of determination and the value of patience! And for inspiring me to make the very most of the chances life has granted me.

Contents

Acknowledgements

I would like to thank all of my colleagues and clients at The CV Centre, both present and past. Without them it would clearly not have been possible for me to write *The Interview Book*. In particular, I would like to thank Susan Staley, who has closely supported me in the production of this book. I would also like to thank Linda Savill, Katy Wilson and Amanda Jackson.

I would additionally like to thank Richard Day at Beaufort Web Design for his significant contribution to the online elements of this book.

Special thanks also go to the team at Pearson, in particular Samantha Jackson, Caroline Jordan and Daniel Culver. I couldn't have had better publishers behind me. Assistance in checking and correcting the text was also provided by Don Elkins, Elisabeth Elkins, Malcolm Innes and Michael Staley.

Finally, I would like to thank Delphine Vaucanson for her love and support and her toleration of my frequently working very excessively long hours!

Introduction

Dear Reader,

'Why do some people almost always get the job they want?'
Because they know precisely how to *truly excel* at interview!

Once your CV has been prepared and you have sent off your applications, the next stage to focus on, in securing the job you want, is the interview phase.

I successfully coach my clients day in day out to truly excel at interview. This enables me to bring you the very best of what I have learned – helping you to excel at interview yourself.

So you've been invited for interview?

Your CV has been successful and you have been invited for interview; what next? People often think, well, I'll just turn up and be myself – which is fine, but it won't get you the job! You need to plan and prepare for an interview as you are still up against many other applicants and this is your key opportunity to make an impact. Your CV has helped you get your foot in the door; you need to do the rest!

Why is it so important to plan and prepare?

The best person for the job, in terms of the right skills, experience and achievements, doesn't always pass the interview. The best person for the job doesn't always get the job. Sometimes the most able candidates on paper can really shoot themselves in the foot when they actually get to the interview.

The interview is one of the most critical points in the job search process. While you might look great on paper, you need to subsequently prove that in front of a recruiter. Many other factors that are not directly related to the person's ability to do the job are going to be picked up in the interview.

You've got the skills; now you need to demonstrate clearly that you'll be a good fit with your future co-workers and employers – and it's so easy to sabotage this valuable opportunity if you're unprepared.

On average, there are likely to be at least five other candidates being interviewed for the same vacancy. So, everything else being equal, that gives you, at the most, a 20 per cent chance of getting the job. But there's so much you can do to improve your odds of success and, in *The Interview Book*, I'll help to give you that winning edge.

What can this book do to help you?

In *The Interview Book* I will show you how to develop a winning strategy – planning and preparing for every eventuality, and learning how to handle every possible kind of interview, from a brief chat over the telephone through to a trip to an assessment centre.

I'll take you through plenty of real interview questions and make sure you know how to avoid clichés and really make an impact when handling both the classic questions – and the really tough ones that interviewers can throw at you.

And I'll take you beyond the interview to discuss what you need to do to close the deal to your advantage.

You'll find this book useful whether you are trying to land your first job, returning to the workplace after a career break or simply looking to take another step up the career ladder. *The Interview Book* condenses the same proven methodology I use every day with my clients and contains all the tips and – dare I say it – tricks, that you need. I will cut through all the debate and opinion about interviews and show you what really works from the recruiter's point of view – what I have *proved* to work.

The CV Centre website

I have made a commitment to readers of this book to provide numerous features to complement the book online at The CV Centre's website: **http: //www.ineedacv.co.uk**. I also provide you with the opportunity to make contact with me and my team directly. Features include:

- The CV Centre Forum: you can exchange comments and ideas with other readers and also pose specific questions directly to members of The CV Centre team, including myself.
  http://www.ineedacv.co.uk/forum
- The CV Centre Blog: a regular column, drawing on specific questions, topics and problems raised in the forum and elaborating on them in detail.
  http://www.ineedacv.co.uk/blog
- The CV Centre Tools: free CV review, job vacancy database, templates to download, etc.

As a reader of *The Interview Book,* access to all these tools and facilities is free. Throughout the book you will be given special links taking you directly to the pages in question.

Special Offer

I have also prepared a special offer for you. If, after reading this book, you decide you would like a coaching session with myself or a member of my team, I'll be giving you a 25 per cent discount on the first 30-minute session.

Simply visit the following page on our site to take advantage of this exclusive offer.

http://www.ineedacv.co.uk/978027372158

Thank you for choosing *The Interview Book*. I have set out to write the most complete and up-to-date guide to interview technique on the market today – a definitive guide to interviews. I trust you will both enjoy it and find it useful. And I look forward to meeting you on our forum should you have any further questions. Or maybe I'll have the opportunity to coach you one-on-one myself.

I really want to help you get the job – and the future – that you want.

James Innes

Kind regards

James Innes
Managing Director
The CV Centre

How to use this book

There's no doubt about it; this book covers a lot of ground.

However, I appreciate that you may well have an interview to attend later today and simply might not have the time to read everything. I have therefore provided a 'fast track' below by listing the top 15 questions that people ask about interviews. This should help you to quickly and easily answer the vast majority of the points that are troubling you.

Once you've found the answers to your questions, before heading off for your interview, do make sure you spare five minutes to read the final chapter, Chapter 32, 'My five top tips to interview success'. If you only had time to read two pages of *The Interview Book*, these are the pages I would most like you to have read. It encapsulates the most important principles that I cover in the book. Make an effort to accommodate all these when preparing for your interview and you'll immediately be well above average.

I'd also recommend that you take time to have a good look at Chapter 19, 'The top ten interview questions'. You are absolutely certain to get asked at least some of these questions (or variations of them) if not the whole lot.

The top 15 questions that people ask me about interviews

Right, if you're short on time and need answers fast then this section is for you.

No, I'm not talking about the questions you *might be asked* at interview. I'm talking about the questions you'd *most like to ask* me about interviews.

The chances are you've got at least one – if not more – of the following questions on your mind.

I have compiled this list based on the questions we most frequently get asked at The CV Centre. It contains the top 15 most common questions concerned job hunters ask about interviews – the questions that come up regularly every single day. If you're reading this book then it's more than likely that you will be asking yourself many of the same questions.

Each question is listed alongside details as to where in this book you can find the answers you are looking for.

All the answers to these questions and many more can be found within *The Interview Book*. And if you have a question to which you can't find the answer then why not visit our online forum:

http://www.ineedacv.co.uk/forum

The top 15 questions

1 What sort of things should I be reading up on before my interview?

Chapter 1 Researching the job

Chapter 2 Researching the organisation

2 What can I do to calm my nerves and be more confident in myself and my abilities?

Chapter 4 Mental preparation

3 What should I wear?

Chapter 5 Presentation

4 What's all this about body language?

Chapter 6 Body language

5 What's really important to remember on the day itself?

Chapter 7 The Big Day

6 How can I make a really strong first impression?

Chapter 8 First impressions count

7 What can I expect to happen at my interview?

Chapter 10 Classic one-on-one interviews

8 How should I handle a panel interview?

Chapter 11 Panel interviews

9 What are competency-based interviews?

Chapter 12 Competency-based interviews

10 How can I prepare for psychometric/aptitude tests?

Chapter 13 Psychometric and aptitude tests

11 What if I've been asked to give a presentation?

Chapter 14 Presentations

12 What is an assessment centre?

Chapter 16 Assessment centres

13 What sort of questions am I most likely to be asked?

Chapter 19 The top ten interview questions

14 How can I prepare myself to cope with any 'tough' questions I might be asked?

Chapter 21 The top 25 tough questions: taking the heat

15 What should I ask when it's time for me to ask my own questions?

Chapter 25 Ending the interview: your own questions

PART 1

PLANNING, PREPARATION AND ORGANISATION: A WINNING STRATEGY

Chapter 1

Researching the job

The key to preventing pre-interview jitters is to prepare yourself thoroughly. We fear what we don't know and what we can't control, yet there is so much you can do to plan and prepare for your interview. Interviews are often seen as a gruelling experience – but they really shouldn't be.

In most cases, you will be notified that you have got through to the interview stage at least a few days in advance. You can use this time to prepare – and the better prepared you are, the fewer your reasons to be nervous.

The first item on your list should be to thoroughly research the job in question.

Researching the job

Not knowing the ins and outs of a job is among the worst blunders you can make in an interview – as is failing to demonstrate to the interviewer how you meet the requirements for the job.

A very large proportion of the questions you can expect to be asked will focus on these two areas:

- your understanding of what the job will entail
- your suitability for fulfilling the demands of the job.

If you are to be able to convince a recruiter that you are right for the role then you obviously need to first get it clear in your own mind why you are right for the role – and you can't do this unless you have properly researched and understood what it will involve.

Information at your fingertips

Your first step should be to go over the job advert, description and/or person specification thoroughly. Most employers (and recruitment agencies) will have provided you with this type of information. Some organisations are kind enough to send out a whole wealth of literature to potential candidates – although most of this will relate to the organisation as a whole, not the particular job for which you are applying. (We'll come on to researching the organisation in the next chapter.)

See how your CV compares with the employer's outline of the role – and try to identify both how and why you are a good match.

TOP TIP

Write it all down and feel free to take that piece of paper with you to the interview as a form of 'cheat sheet'. You may have largely memorised it by the time you get to the interview but it can still be useful to trigger your thought processes should you freeze up during the interview as a result of nerves.

Questions you might be asked

Many interviewers will use either your own CV or the job description/person specification as the agenda for your meeting. These are vital documents and you need to study them carefully. Now is the time to start envisaging what questions you might be asked – and to start drafting rough answers. We'll talk about interview questions very comprehensively later in this book but, for now, you just need to be thinking how you can demonstrate that you meet their needs – and how you can evidence that through appropriate examples.

Questions you'd like to ask

You should also start making a note of any questions about the job that you would like answered at the interview – you have the right to ask questions too! – and there's no shame in having pre-prepared and written down these questions. A prospective employer can't expect a candidate to make an informed decision as to whether to accept a job unless they have all the necessary information to hand.

Chapter 2

Researching the organisation

A number of popular interview questions are designed to probe and assess your knowledge of the organisation to which you are applying. An interviewer will expect you to have done your homework. If you're unprepared and unable to adequately answer these questions then it's going to be a big, black mark on your application.

Just as a lack of knowledge of the job in question will count against you, a lack of knowledge of the organisation will betray a lack of effort on your part. How can a company be sure you really want this job – and that you're really the right candidate for the job – if you know so little about the organisation?

BLOOPER!

One candidate, famously, upon being asked what he could bring to the company, responded with 'What is it that you do again?'

Researching the organisation

Try to find out as much as you can about your prospective employer. The more information you have at your fingertips the better.

The Internet is normally an excellent research tool. Most organisations will have websites where you can read all about their background, structure, products/services, etc. Some will even list biographical details of key employees, maintain archives of press releases, provide downloadable financial accounts, etc. In the space of half an hour you should be able to brief yourself thoroughly.

If your prospective employer has premises that are open to the public – for example a branch on the high street – then it may be worth your while taking the time to drop by and have a closer look. If you're applying to work for a major retail chain and you haven't even set foot inside one of its shops then I'm sure you can see how that might be a problem. If an interviewer asks you about their shops and you have to confess you've never visited one then it'll not only be embarrassing – it'll be extremely damaging to your chances.

Broader background research

Besides researching the organisation itself, you should also try to understand the environment in which it operates. Again, the Internet is a valuable resource. However, specialist trade journals can also yield a wealth of useful information.

- What industry or sector does the organisation operate within?
- How is this industry or sector currently evolving?
- Who are the main players within the industry or sector?

How to use this information

If you've made an effort to research both the organisation and the environment in which it operates then you will immediately have a head start on other candidates – and you haven't even got anywhere near the interview room. Feels good, doesn't it?

Too many candidates at interview know little or nothing about the organisation they are applying to. By demonstrating that you have done at least some preliminary research into the organisation you underline your interest, enthusiasm and motivation.

STATISTIC

Approximately 80 per cent of candidates at interview will have conducted no research whatsoever.

When planning and preparing your answers to potential interview questions, you should try to weave in little snippets of information about the organisation. Show the interviewer that you know what you're talking about. It's bound to impress them.

Being properly briefed will also help you to feel much more confident in yourself. Fear of the unknown is a powerful fear. The more you know about your prospective employer the less nervous you'll be when you turn up on the doorstep.

Questions to ask yourself

For your own benefit, you will also want answers to the following kinds of question:

- What does this organisation have to offer me?
- Are they the right employer for me?
- Will there be sufficient opportunities for career progression?

Thoroughly researching the organisation prior to your interview will give you the answers to some of these questions – and you can fill in any blanks during the interview itself.

Chapter **3**

Travel arrangements and safety considerations

The importance of making appropriate travel arrangements to get to your interview may seem obvious. However, this is frequently a problem for candidates. Being late for an interview – even by only a few minutes – is a very common mistake but it will immediately count against you.

Where?

Where is the employer based? If the employer occupies a number of rooms in separate buildings, it is easy to end up in the wrong place.

You need to plan your route in advance. It may seem obvious but, if you need to get the train, where is the nearest railway station? Sketch yourself a little map or, even better, print one from the Internet. The following is an excellent resource:

WEB LINK http://maps.google.co.uk/

You need to check precisely where it is that you are expected to go and then make doubly sure that you know exactly how to get there.

When?

It is obviously vital for you to find out when the interview is to be held – calculate how long it will take you to get there and make sure that you leave in plenty of time (particularly if you are relying on public transport). You should be aiming to arrive at least ten minutes before the start of your interview – not ten minutes after!

Make sure that you're on time and you'll have an immediate advantage over those who turn up late. It's simple but it's true. Arriving late is consistently cited in surveys as one of the very top reasons that recruiters reject candidates at interview stage.

STATISTIC

Nearly half of recruiters won't give a candidate a job if they are more than ten minutes late for interview – regardless of how well they perform.

It's also important to arrive early in terms of allowing yourself time to relax and compose yourself.

Who?

You need the answers to the following three questions:

- What is the name of your primary contact?
- Who exactly will be interviewing you?
- What are their respective job titles?

If the organisation (or your recruitment agency) hasn't provided you with this information then it's imperative to find it out.

Personal safety

Your personal safety might not even cross your mind when you receive an invitation for an interview. You're probably far more focused on the opportunity the interview presents.

While it is true that the vast majority of job interviews are straightforward in terms of personal safety, it doesn't take a great effort to adhere to a few simple rules:

- First and foremost, always tell a friend, relative or trusted colleague precisely where you are going and what time you are expecting to be back.
- Never agree to be interviewed anywhere other than the organisation's premises or in some other public or official place.
- Try to arrange to have someone collect you if the interview is taking place outside normal office hours, especially if it's after dark. Never let the interviewer drive you home.

Uninvited guests

While it's fine for someone to collect you after an interview, never take anyone with you to an interview. You should always attend an interview alone.

The interviewer is not expecting you to arrive with a guest and won't be pleased if you do, even if you do think they can just wait for you in reception.

Chapter 4

Mental preparation

Most of my clients are understandably nervous about attending job interviews.

We've already talked about preparing yourself on a practical basis; now it's time to talk about your mental preparation. You've got to get yourself into the right frame of mind.

Nerves

Nerves can often be a useful tool for sharpening up your performance. However, if your nerves take over to the extent that they interfere with your ability to come across well at interview, then it's clearly a problem.

Nerves are commonly caused by your having lots of negative thoughts rattling around in your brain. Try to relax, calm your anxious mind and think positive thoughts. Remember: everyone gets nervous to some degree before an interview. It's perfectly normal.

Of course, the better prepared you are, the less likely you are to feel panicky – but you'll never completely eliminate nerves. The secret is to channel your nervous energy and use it to your advantage. Take a deep breath, focus, concentrate and don't let nerves spoil your day. In any case, most professional recruiters are trained to make allowances for the fact that you are likely to be a little on edge.

TOP TIP

Bear in mind that you always feel more nervous than you actually look. Once you realise this, you should feel a lot calmer.

Attending an interview isn't very much different from going on a date really – except that your chances of getting the interviewer naked are probably not very high!

Confidence

Confident people inspire confidence in others; it's almost contagious. If you appear confident that you are able to do the job, the employer is likely to be more inclined to believe that you can.

Confidence is critical to a successful interview. Naturally it is important not to go to the other extreme and appear overconfident or arrogant – which is a surprisingly common mistake. You simply need to appreciate what your strengths are and to value yourself accordingly.

If a prospective employer has invited you for an interview then you obviously have something that appeals to them. Interviews are an expensive and time-consuming process and they wouldn't be making the effort unless they felt you had significant potential.

Enthusiasm

While there's obviously a fine balance here, enthusiasm in an interview is essential – just don't overdo it! Recruiters often find that the person they are interviewing lacks enthusiasm – and this will naturally count against you. Sometimes it might just be due to nerves and shyness – but don't let this happen to you. Be enthusiastic – and show it. If you're not enthusiastic about the role – and about the organisation – then you won't do yourself justice. This is one of the easiest things to get right. Alongside confidence, enthusiasm is a trait that is guaranteed to impress an interviewer.

Show you are motivated. Talk about your work with enthusiasm. Demonstrate that you are keen to do your best.

Tone of voice

Nerves, confidence and enthusiasm will all be reflected in the way you speak. Nerves, stress and pressure will have a negative impact, while confidence, enthusiasm and energy will come across positively.

Take some time prior to your interview to work on your tone of voice. You might feel a little mad talking out aloud to the mirror but it's an exercise that's well worth trying!

Keeping a smile on your face will also help – and we'll cover that in more detail in Chapter 6, 'Body language'.

Chapter 5

Presentation

Presentation, Presentation, Presentation.

The way you physically present yourself will make an impression on an interviewer before you even have a chance to open your mouth.

Present yourself professionally and the interviewer will see you as a professional – but the opposite also applies. Never forget that you are marketing yourself – and the way you present yourself can have an impact on the interviewer that is almost as powerful as what you actually have to say for yourself.

Presentation can make all the difference between success and failure. Image is everything!

The apparel oft proclaims the man

Yes, Shakespeare was right. *Costly thy habit as thy purse can buy!*

In a recent poll, a majority of recruiters cited dressing inappropriately or scruffily as the most damaging mistake a candidate can make in an interview. Candidates with bad breath or unkempt hair are also not uncommon – and often blow their chances of selection before even entering the interview room.

STATISTIC

Research has shown that your interviewer could well have made up their mind about you within just 30 seconds of having met you. Use this to your advantage.

But not expressed in fancy; rich, not gaudy

I'm not going to give you any precise fashion tips; I've seen too many interview books with dodgy and often laughable fashion advice! I'm not David Beckham; everyone is different; fashions change. At the end of the day it's up to you to dress as you deem appropriate.

However, here are some general guidelines I believe you should stick to.

For everyone:

- Make sure that you have an outfit that is smart, presentable – and fits you well.

- Clothes that can be ironed or pressed certainly should be.
- Clean and polish your shoes.
- Wash and brush your hair.
- Cut and file your nails.
- Remove any facial piercings.
- Unless it's really hot, you should generally keep your jacket on.

For the ladies:

- Keep clothes plain and classic in style, avoiding fancy colours, motifs and logos.
- Dress conservatively – skirts shouldn't be too short; dresses shouldn't be too low-cut.
- Keep make-up to a sensible minimum, aiming for fresh but neutral colours.
- Nail polish is recommended but must be simple – and freshly applied.
- Jewellery should be discreet and not overly showy.
- Hair clips and bands, etc. should be kept to a functional minimum.

For the gents:

- For most circumstances, you can't beat a smart, dark suit.
- Remain conservative in your choice of shirt colour – stick to shades of white and blue.
- Keep ties simple. Avoid fancy colours, motifs and logos.
- Get your hair cut. Short hair is generally seen as more professional than long hair.
- Aim for a clean-shaven look. If you have a beard or moustache make sure it is trimmed.
- Limit the amount of jewellery you wear. Avoid earrings.

TOP TIP

Try on your whole outfit before the day of the interview to check that there are no drooping hems, buttons missing, etc.

Disclaimer

The last thing I want is to cause any offence with these guidelines. You may feel you are perfectly within your rights as a man to wear an earring – and no doubt you are. However, it's probably not going to help your chances of successfully passing an interview. My guidelines are necessarily generalised and, at the end of the day, it's really up to your own personal judgement how you choose to present yourself.

BLOOPER!

Some candidates wear so much perfume or aftershave that interviewers have been known to have to open a window!

Surf's up, dude!

Comfortable clothes will make you feel, well ... comfortable. But that doesn't mean you should wear tracksuit bottoms like one candidate did. It may well be that you're hitting the beach after the interview, but it doesn't give you licence to wear flip-flops! You might think you look good in your boob tube – but it sends out all the wrong signals.

Dress appropriately for the circumstances.

Your prospective employer's dress policy may be casual, but save your fashion statements until after you get the job. Fashion makes too many victims. Dress at least as well as you would when actually turning up to do the job – preferably better. Even software engineers and physicists have been known to wear suits to interviews!

Dress to impress.

If you feel that you have made an effort and look good then you will come across as more confident and relaxed.

Lucky underwear

More than half of interview candidates admit to wearing lucky underwear to boost their confidence in an interview

By all means, wear your lucky underwear to the interview but remember that lucky underwear is not going to increase your chances of getting the job – careful preparation will. And if you take matters to extremes and believe that washing your lucky underwear will 'wear off' the luck (and, trust me, some candidates do believe this) then, depending on how little you've washed them and how often you've worn them, be warned that wearing your lucky underwear might actually count against you!

STATISTIC

A staggering 85 per cent of interview candidates take along some sort of lucky trinket, including lucky jewellery, a lucky stone, a lucky pen or even lucky shoes.

Freak accidents

Of course there are the freak accidents – the woman who walked into an interview room with lavatory paper stuck to her shoe and the woman who didn't notice her skirt was tucked into her knickers around the back – and of course the man who managed to get his pants stuck in his trouser zip and had to sit through the entire interview with his pants peeking out through his fly! There's only so much you can do to avoid these sorts of things happening!

Chapter 6

Body language

The fact that you've been selected for interview means that you've obviously made a positive impression on paper. Your next challenge is to build on this by making a positive impression in person.

Recruiters are trained to make informed assessments of candidates, not only based on how they communicate verbally but on how they communicate physically.

Even if your interviewer has received no formal training, they are going to be inherently sensitive to certain nuances of body language – just like the rest of us. It's instinctive.

The importance of body language as a factor in the decision-making process should not be underestimated.

Positive actions

There are a number of positive actions that you can use to your advantage in an interview situation:

- Make and maintain eye contact – without actually staring! Eye contact is essential when trying to convey trust and confidence but should not be overdone as it can come across as aggressive.
- Shake hands firmly – but not to the extent that first aid is required! Seriously, shake someone's hand too firmly and it can imply arrogance and if you deliver a weak handshake it can suggest weakness. This is not just an old wives' tale – it's true. In surveys, recruiters regularly cite getting the handshake wrong as an immediate turn-off.
- Keep your chin up (literally and metaphorically!) – smile with open lips and tilt your head slightly to show that you are attentive.
- Place your hands with your fingertips touching together – which, believe it or not, helps to convey a sense of authority.

Negative actions

There are, of course, an equal number of negative actions.

Some are obvious: You shouldn't pick your nails, pick your nose – or pick any other bodily part for that matter!

And some are less obvious ...

Here are some examples of negative traits and how your body language can give them away:

- defensiveness: crossing your arms
- boredom: feet tapping, playing with your pen, looking down, slouching
- nervousness: fidgeting, thumb-twiddling, playing with your hair
- arrogance/overconfidence: brisk and erect walk, hands clasped behind head
- aggression: postures such as hands on hips and pointing or wagging your index finger
- doubt: rubbing eyes or nose.

Reading the interviewer's own body language

The interviewer's own body language can give you some insight into what they think of what you are saying – for example, if they're getting bored! You can then react to that, for example by changing the subject fast!

TOP TIP

An 'insider' trick is to copy certain aspects of someone's body language. Imitating someone else's body language can have a positive subconscious effect on their impression of you. The theory is that they will feel that you are on the same wavelength as them and automatically become better disposed towards you. You should try to be subtle about it of course – and avoid copying any negative behaviour!

The importance of smiling

I'm not about to suggest you should spend the whole interview grinning like a lunatic but ... smile and the world smiles with you!

Smile at someone and the chances are that they will smile back. Try it. It's human nature; it's a built-in reflex that we have, enabling us to immediately communicate our friendly and peaceful intentions – even at a distance. It's such an innate behaviour that even if you sit by yourself and smile, you'll actually feel better for it! Again, if you don't believe me then try it!

At certain moments during your interview, a big smile is called for – most particularly when you first meet and when you depart. However, you should try to keep a small smile lingering around your lips right the way through the interview – even if the going gets tough. It will definitely have a positive effect on your interviewer's perception of you (firmly proved by psychologists) and you will even feel more positive yourself.

Chapter 7

The Big Day

So, the 'The Big Day' has finally arrived and it's soon going to be time for your interview.

Apparently, more than two-thirds of interview candidates check their horoscope for the day. If you find that reassuring then by all means do so. But try not to read too much into it! It could just end up unnerving you.

I'd suggest you concentrate your efforts on a number of other areas, which I'll run through with you below.

Breakfast and lunch

Whether or not you usually have something to eat for breakfast, make an effort to have breakfast on your interview day. If your interview is not until the afternoon, then you should also make sure you have something to eat for lunch as well.

You might not feel much like eating (that's your nerves getting the better of you) but you definitely want to avoid going into an interview with an empty stomach.

Having breakfast (or lunch) will:

- boost your energy levels and help you to think straight
- settle any butterflies in your stomach/acid indigestion
- stop your stomach from gurgling embarrassingly!

Whilst having something to eat is definitely a good idea, it wouldn't be advisable to have too heavy a meal. That might just send you to sleep!

Setting off

Make sure that you allow yourself enough time to get ready (gather your thoughts, go to the lavatory, check your appearance in the mirror, double-check your appearance in the mirror, etc.).

Also, remember to take the letter inviting you to the interview and any maps, etc. that you might need. Depending on the circumstances, you may also need to take copy (or original) exam certificates, records of achievement, etc. with you.

Try to establish what the weather is likely to do and make sure you're prepared for it. You don't want to arrive soaking wet!

TOP TIP

You should always make sure you take a copy of your CV – or application form – with you so that you can refer to it immediately prior to – and even during – the interview if necessary. Ideally you shouldn't need to refer to it too much; reading through it shortly before the interview should be sufficient to refresh your memory of its contents.

Dutch courage

Avoid alcohol at all costs. If you've planned and prepared properly you won't need any 'Dutch courage'. There are numerous stories of shy or nervous candidates turning up at interview after one drink too many, including a bus driver! It goes without saying that alcohol impairs your judgement.

It's probably best to avoid drinking too much the night before as well. You don't want to turn up for an interview hungover and dehydrated, and suffer from the dreaded 'dry mouth'. It could make it rather difficult to answer the questions!

Conversely, you should of course avoid drinking too much water because you certainly don't want to have to interrupt the interview to go to the lavatory – and going to the lavatory on arrival for your interview or just prior to your departure never makes for a very good impression either.

It's now been fairly conclusively proved that drinking coffee doesn't actually cause dehydration. However, limiting your caffeine intake is advisable nonetheless. You definitely don't want to appear overly manic to your interviewer. If you've ever seen the film *Trainspotting* then you may recall Spud's famous interview! If not then try searching for 'Spud trainspotting interview video' on the Internet and you'll be sure to find a clip.

You should also, of course, avoid any non-prescription drugs.

BLOOPER!

Asked if he would mind undergoing a drugs test, one candidate replied, 'Not at all – I'm happy to test any drugs you like!'

Interview with the vampire?

I would recommend steering clear of garlic, curry and other pungent foods before your interview – or even the night before. They're likely to remain on your breath and, if you sweat when you're nervous (and most of us do), the organic chemicals that cause these odours are likely to ooze out all over your skin and evaporate into the air around you. Best avoided really!

Also, whilst you might feel a greater need for a cigarette than usual, try a nicotine patch for the day instead. Smoke before an interview and the smell will follow you in to the interview room on your breath, your clothes and in your hair. As an ex-smoker myself, I know that nicotine patches don't relieve the craving as effectively as a proper cigarette does – but today is definitely one day when it will be worth the suffering!

Gum chum?

While chewing gum might be a good idea before your interview – to freshen your breath – make sure you discard it before you arrive for the interview. I have interviewed candidates who chewed their way through an interview, and it definitely doesn't make for a good impression. Neither does it make for a good impression to arrive in reception and drop your gum in the bin. Bin it before you even get to the premises.

HELLO?! YES! NO! I'M AT AN INTERVIEW! WHAT?!

- Make sure your mobile phone is switched off before you get to the interview.
- Make sure it stays switched off during the interview.
- Make sure it stays switched off until you have most definitely left the building.
- Make sure you don't forget any of the above!

It's common sense but you'd be surprised how many people forget – or simply don't think about it.

Surveys show that having a mobile phone ring during an interview – or, worse, actually answering a mobile phone during an interview – is a Top 10 reason for a recruiter to reject a candidate. Unless you're applying to work as a Dom Joly lookalike don't even think about leaving your phone switched on.

BLOOPER!

One candidate even answered her phone and then asked if the interviewer would mind leaving his own office because it was a 'private' conversation!

If you do forget to turn your phone off and it subsequently rings during the interview, ignore it (or turn it off as discreetly as possible so as to ensure it doesn't ring again) and apologise profoundly and sincerely to the interviewer. You might just about be able to salvage the situation.

Chapter 8

First impressions count

First impressions are extremely important. Interviewers can reach a decision about a candidate very quickly, so make sure that you walk into that room as if you really want the job. Make a poor first impression and you might not be able to recover from it. How quickly do you sum up someone you've just met? It's probably less than a couple of minutes.

Remember: you never get a second chance to make a first impression!

Taking centre stage

You are literally on show from the moment you arrive at your employer's premises. Your interview starts immediately – so try not to look like you've just arrived for your own execution!

Walk confidently into the building, smile at the receptionist, introduce yourself and explain who it is that you've come to see and why.

TOP TIP

It's always worth being as nice as pie with receptionists; they can have a surprising amount of influence in an organisation, not least because they know absolutely everyone.

In the waiting room

You will more than likely be asked to take a seat and wait for a few minutes while someone comes 'down' to meet you.

There are those who say that you shouldn't sit and that you should remain standing – because this somehow conveys enthusiasm. I don't quite grasp that personally. I feel your time is better spent sitting down, trying to relax and compose yourself. It probably wouldn't hurt to pick up any corporate literature that happens to be lying around and read it, or at least pretend to be reading, with interest. It may in fact help to get you in the right frame of mind.

In any case, research into body language reveals that most people perceive a sitting position as conveying confidence, power and authority. Whenever you were hauled into the headmaster's office at school, who remained seated while you were forced to stand?

First contact

The most likely person to come and collect you is the interviewer themself. However, don't count on it. An assistant could easily be sent. Regardless, you should of course stand up the moment you are approached, move forwards to greet them, smile and deliver a decent handshake. They will introduce themself and you will then know who you are dealing with. Even if it's 'just' an assistant, follow the same rule as for receptionists – be nice to them!

Small talk

On the way to the interview/meeting room it is normal to engage in a bit of light chat as to your health, your journey, the weather, the news headlines – the sorts of things we Brits normally chat about to fill in awkward pauses! Don't let your nerves trick you into babbling. Just respond politely without going into too much detail. But do remember to speak up: a quiet little voice can have the same impact as a weak handshake.

An interviewer is much more likely to look favourably on a candidate with whom they feel they have developed a rapport, so try to be friendly without being overfamiliar.

Places please!

As you enter the interview room you will be invited to sit down. Take your seat, sit up straight and face the interviewer as if you were almost eager for the first question to be asked!

Final impressions matter too

At the end of the interview you will normally be escorted to the exit. Give the interviewer a final handshake, smile and leave with your head held high.

You were on show from the moment you arrived and you remain on show until you are right out of sight. If the stress of it was all too much for you, don't immediately get your fags out of your pocket and light up the moment you're out of the door. And if you think you've done well then don't perform a victory dance on the pavement! Avoid screeching excitedly at someone on your mobile phone. Basically, don't do anything except get yourself away and out of sight as quickly and quietly as possible!

Summary

- The key to preventing pre-interview jitters is to prepare yourself thoroughly.
- In order to convince a recruiter that you are right for a role, you obviously need to first get it clear in your own mind.
- By demonstrating that you have done at least some preliminary research into the organisation you underline your interest, enthusiasm and motivation.
- Never forget that you are marketing yourself – and the way you present yourself is vital. Presentation can make all the difference between success and failure.
- First impressions are extremely important. You never get a second chance to make a first impression.

PART 2

INTERVIEW SCENARIOS: EXPECT THE UNEXPECTED

Chapter 9

Basic principles

Interviews vary enormously. While most people's conception of an interview is a classic one-on-one interview – and that is what most candidates may well be expecting – there are a multitude of possible scenarios:

- classic one-on-one interviews
- panel interviews
- competency-based interviews
- psychometric and aptitude tests
- presentations
- group interviews
- assessment centres
- distance interviews.

The interview may be a quick, informal chat across a crowded office or it could involve a panel of interviewers all firing questions at you. You may be asked to sit an aptitude test or prove that you have the necessary skills for the job – a typing test for example. There may even be group activities with other candidates, designed to see how you perform in a team situation.

Often, candidates fail to perform to the best of their abilities because they were thrown into a situation they were not expecting.

The answer?

You can't prepare for every eventuality, but you can certainly prepare for most – and in the following chapters I will cover all the most likely scenarios.

Second and third interviews

Generally, you will only be expected to attend one interview. However, it is important for you to be aware that many employers will require a second interview – or even a third.

The advice in this book applies equally to all interviews – whether your first, second or third. The basic principles remain the same.

You shouldn't necessarily expect that each of the interviews will be of the same type though. Your first interview might be by telephone, followed by a panel interview and ending up with an assessment centre for your third interview. Regardless of the exact scenario, second and third interviews are generally more intensive and detailed.

There's nothing to worry about though. If you've planned and prepared for all the following possible interview scenarios then you should be able to sail through the process, no matter how many interviews you are subjected to.

You should also find that the first interview gives you some idea of areas you will need to be prepared for in your second or third interviews.

Chapter **10**

Classic one-on-one interviews

Mano a mano.

Swords at dawn.

Many candidates, faced with a one-on-one interview, get the strong sensation that they are going into a duel!

Their major mistake is to believe that all the power lies with the interviewer sitting there across the table.

You should always remember that an interview is a two-way process – a two-way process of recruiter and candidate learning more about each other. It's just as much about whether or not they will make a suitable employer as whether or not you will make a suitable employee.

You are of course there to sell yourself. But you're also there to assess your prospective employer and to see whether or not they can offer you what it is that you want.

Handling different interviewers

Interviewers vary widely in their level of experience, from highly qualified HR professionals all the way down to someone conducting their very first interview. A friend of mine was once interviewed for a position by someone who clearly had never conducted an interview in his life – and she ended up having to turn the tables and lead the interview herself!

In any one-on-one situation it's important to establish a rapport with your interviewer. An interview should be a friendly – but professional – discussion. You might not enjoy the experience; the other person might not enjoy the experience! But the more enjoyable you can make it, the better the likely outcome.

Friendly but professionally detached

While rapport is important, being too intimate or 'matey' with the interviewer is definitely to be avoided. You need to keep a certain professional distance.

Many people instinctively try to be humorous in order to break the ice in tense or awkward situations but jokes are generally out of place at interviews.

BLOOPER!

The candidate who said he smoked weed when asked what he did in his spare time and the candidate who said that a threesome was his greatest achievement most probably thought they were building rapport with the interviewer by being witty and amusing. But did it get them the job? No!

The importance of mock interviews

Undertaking mock interviews with someone you trust is probably the very best way to practise your interview technique – apart of course from sitting a number of real interviews.

Try to find a friend, family member or trusted colleague who can sit down with you for 30 minutes or so and hit you with some of the questions we'll be covering later in this book.

It's all very well to sit down by yourself and write out 'perfect' answers to all the common questions but it's certainly not the same as having a real, live human being sit opposite you and ask you the questions face to face.

Chapter 11

Panel interviews

A panel interview is an extension of the classic one-on-one interview. The difference is very obvious – instead of being faced with one interviewer, you will be faced with two, three or more.

I find that candidates are normally considerably more nervous about attending a panel interview than they would be if they were simply attending a one-on-one interview. However, there's really no need to be.

In this chapter I'll cover the few simple issues you need to bear in mind when dealing with a panel interview and you'll see that there's really nothing to worry about.

Because two, three or more heads are better than one, you can definitely expect your panel interview to be quite intense – but, provided you've prepared thoroughly, there shouldn't be anything you can't cope with.

The panel

The first step is to understand who is on the panel and what role each one is fulfilling – why are they there? Most panels won't expect you to be telepathic; they'll normally be polite enough to introduce themselves and you should be able to easily deduce for what reason each person is on the panel.

A panel will always have a 'chair' – a person who is ostensibly 'in charge' of proceedings and who will be responsible for guiding the overall direction of the interview. They will normally be easy to identify right from the very start – and, if not, bear in mind that they have a tendency to sit either in the middle of the other interviewers or on their own at the head of the table.

TOP TIP

While you should always take a copy of your CV or application form with you to an interview, if you're attending a panel interview then take several copies with you. It's very common to find poorly prepared interviewers sharing a copy – and if you've brought along extra copies for them then it's bound to impress.

The chair will be assisted in questioning you by the other panel members – who could be there for a variety of reasons. Panel interviews are popular where it is not considered practical for one, single person to effectively assess your suitability for a role. A typical three-person panel could, for example, consist of a department manager acting as chair, assisted by your prospective line manager and perhaps a prospective colleague to question you on specific, technical issues.

Eyes on the prize

In a one-on-one interview it's simple enough to make an appropriate amount of eye contact with your interviewer. However, in a panel interview you must make an effort to make regular eye contact with all panel members in reasonably equal measure. You must build rapport with each and every one of them. Easier said than done – but eye contact is an excellent start.

You talkin' to me?

Also, in a one-on-one interview there's only one person to whom to give your answers. In a panel interview, when one panel member poses a question, focus attentively on that individual but, when it comes to answering, you must address your answer to all of the panel members.

Don't allow your eyes to flit backwards and forth like a rabbit caught in the headlights. As you start your answer, focus on the panel member who asked you the question but, as you make your points, steer your gaze steadily from one panel member to another – in no particular order. If you're experienced in giving presentations then you'll be familiar with this technique. (I'll talk in detail about presentations in Chapter 14, 'Presentations'.)

Avoid focusing too much of your attention on just one panel member, for example the chair or the person who asks the majority of the questions. All panel members will contribute to reaching a decision on your application – and a quieter, less prominent panel member could easily have a surprising amount of influence. Treat them all as equals.

Time to go

When your panel interview draws to a close, ensure that you smile and thank each of the panel members. Given that it is most likely the chair that will wrap up the interview – and indicate to you that the interview is over – it's a natural reaction to only thank the chair. Avoid this mistake and make one final positive impression on all the interviewers. As I say, you really don't know which one will have the casting vote on your appointment to the role.

Chapter **12**

Competency-based interviews

There's a lot of talk about competency-based interviews, behavioural questioning, evidence-based interviewing, etc. It's all the rage.

You've quite possibly heard of these concepts but you very possibly aren't really sure what they actually mean.

Instead of baffling you with lots of jargon and complicated explanations, what I'd like to do in this chapter is to demystify the idea of competency-based interviews. I know that they're a cause of concern for many of my clients – but once I've outlined what competency-based interviewing really means, it normally takes away a lot of their fear.

What is a competency?

The first issue to address is what is actually meant by the word 'competency'. If you look in a dictionary it will tell you that the word 'competence' means 'the condition of being capable; ability'. The word 'competency' is derived from this.

Competency-based interviewing therefore focuses on analysing your ability to handle certain specific tasks and situations, drawing on a combination of your skills and your experience. It helps the interviewer to answer the following two key questions:

- Can you do the job?
- Do you have what it takes?

By examining your past performance, an interviewer will be aiming to effectively judge your future potential to fulfil the role for which you are now applying.

Competency-based questions

Competency-based questions can take a wide variety of different formats and approaches. Many of the questions I cover later in this book probe and analyse key competencies:

- Can you tell me about a major problem at work that you've had to deal with?
- What techniques do you use to get things done?
- Can you tell me about a time when you have failed to achieve a goal?

- Are you able to make difficult decisions and tough choices?
- Can you tell me about a major project you have successfully completed?
- How did you cope with the most difficult colleague you've ever had?
- Can you give me an example of when you have successfully coached a member of your team?

Answering competency-based questions

I'll deal with how to handle these particular questions in detail in later chapters. For now, I just need to emphasise the importance of using examples from your own experience to illustrate your answers. Some questions will specifically demand an example, e.g. 'Can you give me an example of when you have successfully coached a member of your team?' Others won't ask for an example but you'll be expected to give one anyway if your answer is to have any validity, e.g. 'Are you able to make difficult decisions and tough choices?'

The interviewer is looking for you to tell a brief story describing the situation, explaining your behaviour – and highlighting the benefits of your actions. It's no good just saying you possess certain abilities; you need to prove it. Competency-based questions quickly expose any fakes.

Identifying required competencies

Competency-based interviewing is now such an integral part of most interviews that, apart from defining it in this chapter, I haven't treated it separately within this book. I have scattered examples of competency-based questions throughout my lists of the most popular interview questions.

However, my examples are necessarily generalised. In order to prepare properly for your own interviews you will need to identify the specific competencies your prospective employer requires.

Back in Chapter 1, 'Researching the job', I emphasised how important it is to thoroughly study any job description or person specification you have. This should enable you to identify most, if not all, of the key competencies for which an interviewer is going to be seeking evidence. And you should try to establish the perfect example (and preferably more than one example) for each and every one of their criteria.

Follow-up questions

While you should always endeavour to answer each question comprehensively, you can expect a skilled interviewer to hit you with a barrage of follow-up questions. There are only a certain number of different competencies required for the average job and your interviewer is going to want to question you very thoroughly on each one. But if you've carefully prepared and thought through your examples in advance, then their follow-up questions should be easy enough to tackle.

TOP TIP

They will, of course, be looking for weaknesses in your answers and flaws in your arguments, so do stay on the ball and be careful you're not tripped up.

A level playing field

Whilst competency-based questions can – and will – crop up in almost any interview, some employers will have a very formal policy of competency-based interviewing. It's an increasingly popular technique.

This normally means that they will establish in advance what the key competencies are that they are looking for, and they will design a series of questions to help them determine which candidates are best able to fulfil these. In such interviews, all candidates will normally be asked exactly the same set questions in the same sequence (often with a variety of follow-up questions). It's considered to be one of the fairest – and most thorough – selection techniques available.

Whenever you hear someone referring to a competency-based interview, this is generally what they mean.

Not so complicated after all, is it?

Chapter 13

Psychometric and aptitude tests

Most readers will be familiar with the idea of psychometric and aptitude tests, even if you haven't necessarily been subjected to one yet. In this chapter I'm going to give you a brief outline of the various different types of test an employer is likely to roll out. This sort of testing is surprisingly common – and its popularity is on the increase.

STATISTIC

Over 75 per cent of FTSE 100 companies use some form of psychometric or aptitude testing in their recruitment processes.

The chances are that you will run up against one test or another at some stage in your career, so it's important to have an idea of what to expect. For unprepared candidates, such tests can represent a considerable challenge.

The major types of psychometric and aptitude tests I'll be talking about are:

- personality tests/questionnaires
- verbal reasoning
- numerical reasoning
- spatial and diagrammatic reasoning
- mechanical comprehension/aptitude.

Personality tests/questionnaires

A personality test is normally a series of multiple-choice questions which assess you on how you respond to – or feel about – a given situation. They're normally carefully designed so that you can't 'game' them, i.e. identify which of the responses is 'right' – and you shouldn't see such tests in terms of right and wrong anyway. Everybody has a different personality. The employer simply wants to gain some deeper insight into your own personality – the goal being to judge how close a match you are to the needs of the role for which you are applying. My advice is always to answer all questions as truthfully as possible.

Verbal reasoning

Verbal reasoning tests are designed to assess how well your brain handles, understands, processes, analyses and interprets language. They will include questions testing your spelling and grammar, as well as questions which identify whether you can spot synonyms, antonyms, analogies, etc.

Numerical reasoning

Numerical reasoning tests are the numerical equivalent of verbal reasoning tests. You're not expected to have studied mathematics to a high level; the concepts involved are all relatively simple and certainly shouldn't require a calculator. You will be expected to perform simple mental calculations and identify patterns and sequences. Other questions may give you a graph or chart and probe your understanding of it.

Spatial and diagrammatic reasoning

Spatial and diagrammatic reasoning is classic IQ test territory. You will be shown a variety of different shapes and patterns, and be expected to identify differences, commonalities and/or deduce matching members of a set. Questions frequently include 3D images represented in 2D and are designed to test how able you are to visualise an image – to project the image in your mind's eye – and to then manipulate that image. On a more practical level, questions could test your ability to follow a map or street plan.

Mechanical comprehension/aptitude

Tests probing your mechanical comprehension are clearly much less abstract than other aptitude tests – and are only likely to be given to candidates whose work has a distinct mechanical element. Such tests are designed to assess your ability to handle physical and mechanical principles – levers, pulleys, gearing, circuitry, etc.

General tips for psychometric and aptitude tests

Most tests will be delivered under 'exam conditions' – with a specific time limit set for their completion. I'm not saying you should rush though; keeping your cool and avoiding silly mistakes are essential.

As in any exam, carefully observe any instructions you are given – and, most importantly, make sure that you read each question carefully!

Getting in some practice

The best way to prepare for psychometric and aptitude tests is to actually practise them – and we've put together a set of free online tools which will help you to get some practice on all these different types of test.

WEB LINK http://www.ineedacv.co.uk/psychtests

Brilliant Psychometric Tests and *Brilliant Tactics to Pass Aptitude Tests*

Psychometric and aptitude testing is a big subject – and goes way beyond the scope of this book. If you would like to learn more about these sorts of test then please take a look at the following comprehensive books on the subject:

Brilliant Psychometric Tests
Brilliant Tactics to Pass Aptitude Tests

You can order copies via the following page on our website:

WEB LINK http://www.ineedacv.co.uk/brillianttests

Chapter 14

Presentations

In many lines of work, the ability to give powerful presentations is a key skill. As a consequence, it is very common for organisations to request that candidates prepare a presentation for delivery at their interview.

You'll normally only be asked to give a brief presentation – but you'd better make sure you get it right. It's an excellent opportunity to demonstrate your ability to organise yourself, plan, prepare and communicate effectively.

Preparation

In most circumstances, an employer will be decent enough to warn you that you'll be expected to give a presentation. This gives you plenty of time to carry out any necessary research, write, memorise and practise your presentation.

TOP TIP

Make sure your presentation follows a clear and logical structure, beginning with a suitable introduction and closing with an appropriate conclusion; it's always the beginning and the ending of a presentation that gets the most attention.

Usually, you will be given a specific topic for the presentation as well as a suggested length – and it is of course essential to adhere to any such guidelines.

However, a recruiter may really put you to the test by surprising you on the day with an invitation to give a presentation. In this situation, you can only really be expected to deliver a presentation on a topic you're familiar with – so pre-empt this and, if giving presentations forms part of your job description, have a brief presentation ready regardless of whether or not you've been specifically asked to do so.

Delivery

Nerves are probably the biggest enemy you face when delivering a presentation. You're up there at the front all alone with everyone staring at you!

It's a natural instinct for you to feel threatened by this. However, bear in mind that members of the audience are (normally!) on your side and that they are not your enemy – your nerves are. Don't let your nerves win the battle – because it'll reflect immediately in your tone of voice.

TOP TIP

Speak confidently – slightly slower, slightly louder and slightly more deeply than you would normally do so – and articulate each syllable clearly.

Cue cards

Many presenters, myself included, rely on cue cards to help them through their presentation.

Reading from a script is totally unacceptable and, while you should make an effort to memorise as much of your presentation as possible, memorising it verbatim is likely to result in a fairly stiff and stilted delivery.

By using cue cards you can identify the next point you wish to make with a quick downward glance, helping you to spend most of your time maintaining eye contact with your audience.

Eye contact

Eye contact is essential to effective communication. If you've got an audience in front of you then don't focus too much on any one person – move your gaze randomly around the room and aim to make brief eye contact with everyone. Once you've established eye contact, they're a lot more likely to listen to what you have to say. You may even find that they nod their head in agreement!

Physical gestures

Whilst it's normally fine to walk up and down a little bit, you should avoid pacing the floor excessively. Likewise, it's fine to gesture with your hands –

but try to keep it within reasonable limits. You want to convey the impression of someone who is calm and in control – even if you do have a swarm of butterflies in your stomach!

Visual aids

You should be notified in advance whether or not you are expected to use any visual aids – for example a PowerPoint slideshow. If it's not specified then there's nothing to be lost in asking – a PowerPoint presentation is always more powerful than a straightforward verbal presentation. It also gives you an opportunity to demonstrate your proficiency with PowerPoint.

Practice makes perfect

The secret to a successful presentation is practice. Practice reciting your presentation by yourself, practice in front of the mirror and practise in front of a friend.

The more you practise your presentation, the more confident you will become.

Q&A

As you finish your presentation, it is of course expected that you will ask members of your audience whether they have any questions. You should endeavour to anticipate the type of questions you are likely to be asked and have prepared rough answers in advance.

Finally, it's always a nice touch to thank your audience for listening.

Chapter 15

Group interviews

A group interview is defined as an interview in which multiple candidates attend and are assessed simultaneously. The candidates not only get to meet each other but are actually expected to work together on a variety of different tasks. You will be carefully observed and your behaviour will be noted in detail.

Why a group interview?

What are the employer's motivations in interviewing candidates in a group context rather than one-on-one? It could be a time-saving exercise or it could be because they place above-average importance on teamwork – or it could be both. Whatever you think their motivations might be, you should assume that the organisation is indeed looking to identify how you work within a team – what role you naturally fulfil.

What role do you fulfil?

Look at it this way: what role do they want you to fulfil?

Are they looking for a leader? Are they looking for someone who brings out the best in others? Are they looking for the person who generates the ideas or the person who is a dab hand at putting new ideas into practice?

Establish in your own mind what sort of a team player they want you to be and it will help to guide your behaviour.

Maybe you are applying for a role as a team leader – but this doesn't mean that you have to be utterly overbearing and demonstrate to everyone, at all costs, that you're the boss. Is the employer looking for a fascist dictator? The loudest, brashest, pushiest candidate is rarely the one selected.

You can demonstrate that you work well within a group without aggressively taking the lead.

Working well within a group means listening, co-operating, communicating, generating ideas and solutions. Do you help the group to achieve its objectives or are you more of a hindrance?

TOP TIP

Don't be so loud that you drown everyone else out. Conversely, don't be so quiet that nobody even notices you!

Group activities

There are two main types of activity you are likely to encounter at a group interview:

- verbal activities
- physical activities.

In a verbal group interview, the group will typically be given a topic (or topics) to discuss, debate and reach a conclusion on. A chair may be appointed by the interviewer (or the interviewer may themselves chair the discussion) or you may all be expected to contribute equally.

Alternatively, you could be assigned role-play exercises, working in small groups of two or more to act out carefully designed scenarios – which could be related to the job on offer or could be of a more abstract, psychological nature.

It's also a popular technique to ask each candidate to give a brief presentation to the other candidates. Please refer back to the previous chapter for detailed advice on how to handle presentations.

In a physical group interview, activities can vary widely. You may be expected to plan, design and/or physically construct something, or otherwise solve a problem or puzzle. Expect the unexpected.

The other candidates

You're going to spending a few hours – maybe a whole day – with other candidates. While you might, quite reasonably, see them as competition, there's no reason to treat them as enemies. On the contrary, you will be assessed on your ability to get on with and to work with these people – so aim to be friendly and communicative right from the start. Make friends, not enemies. Remember that you're a team.

Under the spotlight

You will be closely observed throughout the day. That might sound stressful but try to keep calm – everyone is in the same boat and they're probably all just as nervous as you.

Key factors on which you will be assessed include communication, initiative, motivation, determination and the ability to function effectively under pressure.

From the moment you arrive to the moment you leave you'll be under the spotlight.

Chapter 16

Assessment centres

Most job hunters will never have heard of an assessment centre. It conjures up an image of a concrete bunker in the middle of a forest where you spend your days tackling assault courses and having your face shoved in the mud – at least that's the image that sprang to my mind when I was first invited to attend an assessment centre!

As it happens, this image couldn't be much further from the truth. For a start, an assessment centre generally isn't a 'centre' at all. It's a term used to describe an event that will commonly take place at an organisation's normal premises – and is unlikely to last more than one day. It doesn't involve assault courses either; it's normally just a mishmash of other, better-known interview scenarios.

Assessment centres are increasingly popular with employers so you need to know what to expect.

What to expect at an assessment centre

All of the interview scenarios I've described so far could come into play at an assessment centre.

You could have a one-on-one interview. You could have a panel interview. You will certainly undergo group interviews.

You may be faced with aptitude tests, psychometric tests, be expected to give a presentation ...

You have to be prepared for all of this – and more.

How to prepare for an assessment centre

The best advice I can give is to be prepared for all the scenarios I have covered in the previous chapters. In particular, you need to be ready to handle group interviews – since these will occupy a large proportion of your time at an assessment centre.

There are also many other tests an employer may use to gauge your capabilities, one of the more popular being what is known as 'in-tray' or, increasingly, 'e-tray'.

The concept is very straightforward. You will be presented with a 'typical' in-tray (or email inbox), containing various items that require your attention. The goal is to ensure that you prioritise your in-tray effectively and take appropriate action to deal with each item – whether that involves actioning it yourself, delegating it or postponing it. And you'll normally be up against the clock. It's just like real life!

TOP TIP

If this all sounds a little nutty to you then keep that to yourself. Employers can take these sorts of exercise very seriously indeed!

Another favourite is the 'case study' where you will be presented with details of a realistic situation you are likely to encounter at work, and will be expected report back your thoughts, findings and recommendations, either by way of a written report or in a verbal presentation.

Do employers really go to all this trouble?

Yes, they most certainly do!

Assessment centres are popular with many large corporations and are particularly used to assist in graduate recruitment drives. They are also used in the public sector, for example the police force.

Delivering an assessment centre is certainly a major undertaking on an employer's part – but it's a very effective technique for them to thoroughly assess a large number of candidates in a short space of time. It enables them to determine, with some confidence, which of those it will be worth investing further in.

Chapter **17**

Distance interviews

Of course, there's no rule that says you have to attend in person for an interview.

Telephone interviews have been commonplace for decades and, with the advent of technologies such as video-conferencing and the Internet, an employer at one end of the country can now easily and immediately interview a potential employee at the other end.

I call such interviews 'distance' interviews and we'll look at how you should handle them in this chapter.

Telephone interviews

Telephone interviews are most commonly used as a shortlisting technique, to whittle down a large number of applicants to a final short list that will be called in for face-to-face interviews. As such, they are more commonly used for first interviews, rather than second or third interviews. However, if you are widely geographically separated from your interviewer then it may be more convenient to conduct the entire process by telephone. It all depends on the employer.

A telephone interview is not really very different from a classic one-on-one interview. The main difference is that you won't, of course, have any visual cues – and neither will they. Issues such as dress sense and body language are immediately irrelevant but most of my other interview advice still applies.

In particular, you need to concentrate on articulating clearly and getting your tone of voice right. The interviewer might not be able to see you smiling but they will be able to hear it in your voice – and they'll also be able to hear a frown!

BLOOPER!

When I was very much younger than I am today, I allowed myself to be interviewed by telephone with my rather rude African Grey parrot within earshot! And one indignant interviewer reported to a survey that he once had a candidate flush the lavatory on him during a telephone interview!

Do be careful of background noises and try to conduct the interview somewhere calm and quiet, rather than on a busy street corner! You should especially avoid eating, drinking, smoking or chewing gum during the interview – as all of these will be distinctly audible. The only exception to this would be for you to take an occasional sip of water to stop your mouth drying up.

Whilst there's nothing wrong with taking a copy of your CV (or application form) or other notes into any interview, a telephone interview makes this much easier. You can lay out all your papers neatly in front of you, so you can put your finger on the precise document you need at a moment's notice:

- CV or application form
- job advert, description or person specification
- a list of the key selling points you want to make
- a list of the questions you would like to ask
- diary or calendar to schedule a follow-up interview.

Whilst it's always better if the interviewer doesn't know that you're referring to notes, it is much more socially acceptable to refer to papers when you are on the phone than when you are sitting face to face in a formal interview setting.

TOP TIP

It will also be much easier for you to take notes yourself – especially if you have a hands-free or loudspeaker facility on your telephone, so that both your hands are free. By taking brief notes as you go along, you can rely on them later when attending a second or third interview – or even use them to help prepare yourself for other interviews.

If the interviewer has arranged to call you:

- Ensure you provide them with the correct telephone number.
- Ensure you are fully prepared and ready to answer at the designated time.
- Ensure that nobody else answers the call.

If the interviewer has asked you to call them:

- Ensure you have the correct telephone number.

- Ensure you call at precisely the time they have designated.
- Ensure you leave a message if you are unable to get through.

Video-conferencing and webcam-based interviews

More and more employers are looking to harness tools such as video-conferencing and the Internet to facilitate the interviewing process.

If meeting in person is impractical (or, for whatever reason, undesirable) then, provided both you and your interviewer have access to appropriate technology, you might find yourself expected to handle such an interview.

First and foremost you need to ensure you fully understand how to use the technology in question. It will not create a good impression if you agree to an interview of this nature and then struggle to deal with the technology.

Apart from this, such interviews are very little different from 'traditional' interviews. You will be in full view of the interviewer (or interviewers) so dress appropriately, maintain a reasonable level of eye contact, smile, articulate clearly – and behave precisely as you would in any other interview.

Because you will be responsible for controlling your own environment, make sure that nobody disturbs you during the interview. If somebody walks in on you during the interview then it is going to reflect very badly on you. This also means switching mobile phones to silent mode and taking other phones off the hook.

Summary

- Often, candidates fail to perform to the best of their abilities because they were thrown into a situation they were not expecting.
- You can't prepare for every eventuality but you can certainly prepare for most.
- In any one-on-one situation it's important to establish a rapport with your interviewer. An interview should be a friendly – but professional – discussion.

- You should always remember that an interview is a two-way process – a two-way process of recruiter and candidate learning more about each other.
- Undertaking mock interviews with someone you trust is probably the very best way to practise your interview technique.

PART **3**

INTERVIEW QUESTIONS – AND THEIR ANSWERS!

Chapter 18

Basic principles

Obviously, no one can know exactly what questions will be asked at interview but there are certain topics that will almost certainly come up.

However, before we start looking at some of the questions you might be asked, I'd like to cover some important ground rules.

Listen!

It's actually surprisingly easy for your thoughts to stray elsewhere and for you to fail to listen properly to a question. You're in a stressful situation and you have a lot on your mind; it's perfectly possible to get distracted. If you do fail to hear a question properly then don't be afraid to ask the interviewer to repeat the question. It's not ideal but it's certainly better than your failing to fully answer the question – or guessing at what you've just been asked, going off at a tangent and giving the answer to a totally different question!

It's also possible that you might fail to understand a question the first time around. Again, don't be afraid to ask the interviewer to repeat or to clarify the question. At the very least it gives you valuable extra thinking time. But don't make a habit of it!

Try to understand the meaning behind the question

Why have they asked you this question? What is it they are trying to find out?

I wouldn't go so far as to say that all interview questions have hidden meanings, but it is true that the intentions of the interviewer might not immediately be apparent from the question. If you can work out the meaning behind the question then you are at least 80 per cent of the way towards determining the optimum answer.

There are three key areas that interviewers will be considering in their attempts to match a vacancy with the best possible candidate:

- Can you do the job? Do you have what it takes?
- Will you do the job? (Or will you just go through the motions?)
- Do you fit in with the other employees and the organisation as a whole?

All of their questions will address one of these three areas in one way or another. Therefore, in trying to understand the meaning behind any particular question you need to first identify which of the above areas the interviewer is trying to tackle.

Beyond that, you need to make sure you see the world from the interviewer's point of view. When asking you a particular question, what exactly is going through their mind?

Different types of question

As well as questions probing different areas, there are also different ways in which interviewers might phrase their questions. You need to be aware of the different techniques they will use because it will naturally impact on the way you answer.

In general terms, most questions can be classified as either 'open' or 'closed'.

A 'closed' question is one which can be answered very quickly – often with just one word:

- Are you creative?
- Do you thrive under pressure?
- Are you a risk-taker?
- Do you have sales experience?

An 'open' question, on the other hand, is one that will force a lengthier answer:

- In what ways would you say that you are creative?
- Can you tell me about a time when you were under significant pressure and how you handled it?
- How do you feel about taking risks?
- Can you tell me about your sales experience?

A good interviewer will normally ask mainly open questions – because these are the questions that will extract the most useful information from you. Conversely, a poor interviewer is likely to ask you a much higher proportion of closed questions.

Regardless of the type of question (or interviewer) you're faced with, you should always avoid 'yes' and 'no' answers to questions unless you're sure it's appropriate – because they tend to be conversation stoppers.

TOP TIP

A single-word answer doesn't give you any scope whatsoever to sell yourself. It's consequently of no benefit either to yourself or to the interviewer. If an interviewer does ask you a closed question, then don't let their inexperience as an interviewer jeopardise your chances of getting your message across. Rework the question in your own mind so that you are actually answering an open form of the question.

Leading questions

Another type of question you are likely to encounter is the 'leading' question:

- What character flaws do you have?
- Why haven't you achieved more in your career?
- You must surely have more than one weakness?

You can see that these questions, whilst open, nevertheless lead you down a very specific path. The interviewer isn't asking you whether or not you have any character flaws; in delivering a leading question they are making it clear they have inherently assumed that you do indeed have character flaws. Leading questions are definitely something you need to keep a close lookout for.

You should also note that a leading question doesn't always have to be an open question. By posing you a leading question which is also a closed question an interviewer can really put you on the spot:

- I think you're overqualified for this job. Don't you?

But don't worry – because I'll show you how to deal with this in Chapter 21, 'The top 25 tough questions: taking the heat'.

Funnel interviewing

A final interviewing technique I'd like to make you aware of is so-called 'funnel' interviewing.

In funnel interviewing, an interviewer will first pose you a very general question about a topic (potentially lulling you into a false sense of security) before following up their original question with more and more precise questions (often based on your previous answers) on the same topic until you are talking about precisely what interests them.

It's a popular interrogation technique! But it's not normally as frightening as it sounds. It all depends on the interviewer. Generally their supplementary questions will follow a fairly mundane sequence, starting with the favourite, 'Can you give me an example?'

The secret to handling this technique is simply to be aware of it and to make sure that you don't let the interviewer force you into revealing anything that's not to your advantage.

Engage brain before opening mouth! (EBBOM)

Think before you speak!

Pause to give yourself the necessary time to construct an answer, so that you answer the question to the best of your ability. If you've prepared properly – and both this and the following chapters should help you to do just that – then it's unlikely any question will come as too much of a shock to you. You should already have an answer more or less ready.

However, if you're taken aback by the question then do give yourself a few seconds before starting to respond. That should be just long enough to get your head around the question and will make a big difference to the quality of your answer.

Keep your answer on track

Make sure that you answer questions fully without waffling or chattering on unnecessarily. Nervousness can all too easily cause you to say too much and to give too much away.

Besides your own nervousness, another reason you are likely to say more than you should is an interviewing technique whereby the interviewer waits for you to finish your answer and then doesn't immediately follow up with another question. They just sit there silently. It's human nature for you to then carry on talking – either by elaborating on your existing answer or by rephrasing your answer – so as to fill the awkward silence.

This is a technique popular with sales negotiators, because forcing someone to say more than they originally intended to say will generally weaken their position. It's also exactly the same technique used by psychotherapists. They are trained to say very little because this forces you to say more – and hence to open up and disclose more. While this might be very useful for someone undergoing psychotherapy, it's likely to cause you to come unstuck in an interview. Be aware of this technique and don't fall into the trap.

An interviewer is especially likely to adopt this tactic after a question such as, 'What are your weaknesses?' The more they can keep you talking, the more you're likely to reveal.

Back up your answers with real-life examples

Wherever possible you should try to integrate real-life examples into your answers rather than just speaking hypothetically. Flagging up specific, relevant examples from your own experience is an ideal way of reinforcing your points in the interviewer's mind.

TOP TIP

If the interviewer asks you a straightforward question without specifically requesting you to give an example, then don't hesitate to be proactive and give an example anyway.

I've already made the point that many interviewers will start with a simple question and then probe the topic further by following up with another question, such as, 'Can you give me an example?'

If you pre-empt this by illustrating your initial response with an example then it's bound to impress them.

Delivering sound bites

If you ever watch a politician or a senior businessman being interviewed on television then you will notice that they all have a little trick up their sleeve. If they've received any kind of debate or media training then they will be adept at making sure they get their point across regardless of the question being asked.

This is especially so when they're discussing particularly sensitive topics or when confronted with a particularly aggressive interviewer. In his famous interview with politician Michael Howard, interviewer Jeremy Paxman asked exactly the same question ('Did you threaten to overrule him?') a total of 12 times without getting a straight answer!

It's clearly vital that you should not be seen as being this evasive. It didn't do much for Michael Howard's reputation and it won't do much for yours! However, if you are able to subtly steer a question around so as to dodge an issue you are uncomfortable with – and deliver a pre-prepared statement you have been keen to make – then it can be a very effective technique. But use it sparingly!

You may not be answering the precise question you have been asked but you should be addressing the topic that the interviewer has raised. You're simply doing so in the manner that suits you best.

The truth, the whole truth ...

Never lie at interview or say something that you cannot substantiate.

For many candidates their troubles start even before they've been invited for the interview because a large percentage of people seem to think it's permissible to tell a few small porkies when writing their CV. Many think it's acceptable because 'anyone else does it' – and it is a fact that many prospective employers do not check an applicant's information as thoroughly as they perhaps should.

However, I would always strongly caution anyone against telling anything but the truth on their CV. You can easily become unstuck during an interview as a result.

BLOOPER!

One candidate claimed to be fluent in French on his CV and then got quite a shock when he came up against a half-French, half-English interviewer who consequently thought it quite reasonable to conduct the interview in French!

And even before the interview, it's not going to do your nerves much good to be worrying about whether or not you are going to be unmasked as a liar. This is a surprisingly common cause of pre-interview jitters.

STATISTIC

Surveys show that approximately 30 per cent of candidates 'lie' to one degree or another at interview.

It all depends, of course, on how you define 'lie'. 20 per cent engage in a 'significant' lie (the kind where you could later be sacked for gross misconduct as a result) whereas up to 35 per cent include at least one small porky here or there.

But just because 'everyone else does it' it doesn't mean that you should. Not everyone lies – it remains a minority – and it is very questionable whether those that do gain any benefit from it whatsoever.

Whether or not you tell the 'whole' truth though is another matter entirely. Clearly you should always put as positive a spin as possible on matters but it's a fine line – and only you can really be the judge of what is and is not acceptable.

Don't be a parrot

An essential warning to all readers:

I will be giving you example answers to a whole variety of questions but I must emphasise that it is vitally important for you to think through and write out your own answers. Once I have fully explained to you the meaning behind the question and given you my pointers on how to develop your own answer, then it shouldn't be too difficult for you to do so.

My examples are purely there to help illustrate the points made; they're there to act as a guide only and most are unlikely to be relevant to your precise circumstances. It's essential for you to think for yourself and create your own answers; my job is purely to help you achieve that.

This will of course take some time and effort on your part, but it is absolutely vital as your answers must come across as genuine. It's time and effort that will really pay dividends. You'll feel so much more confident.

Too many candidates at interview make the mistake of sounding as if they're reciting from some old-fashioned book on interview technique with a title like *1001 Interview Questions*!

Make sure that you don't fall into this trap yourself. This is really important. There are no universally 'right' answers to interview questions – just answers that are right for *you* – and I will help you to work out what those right answers should be.

Even if you have prepared and memorised your own answers, you should be careful to make sure that your delivery is natural, not stilted – and most importantly doesn't come across as rehearsed. This is especially important with the more difficult and challenging questions. If you don't express any surprise, and answer perfectly and without hesitation, then it's going to look rather suspicious!

Chapter **19**

The top 10 interview questions

Here's my list of what I consider to be the top ten questions you are likely to be asked at interview. You should make sure you think through your answers to all these questions very carefully before getting anywhere near an interview room.

1. Tell me about your work experience – what did you do, what did you enjoy, what were you good at, why did you leave each job?
2. Why have you applied for this vacancy?
3. Why do you wish to leave your current position?
4. Why do you want to work for this organisation?
5. What are your strengths?
6. What are your weaknesses?
7. What has been your greatest achievement – in your personal life as well as in your career?
8. What can you, above all the other applicants, bring to this job?
9. Where do you see yourself in five years' time?
10. You've mentioned *x* under 'Interests and Activities' on your CV. Can you tell me a bit more about that?

You are absolutely certain to get asked at least some of these questions (or variations of them) if not the whole lot.

I could add an eleventh question to the list: 'And do you have any questions for me/us?' There aren't many interviews that conclude without this question being asked. But we'll come to that in Chapter 25, 'Ending the interview: your own questions'.

For now, let's concentrate on the questions above.

We'll look at them one by one, alongside possible alternatives and other closely related questions. We'll analyse the interviewer's intentions in asking you the question – the meaning behind the question – and we'll discuss how best you can answer it.

Top question: can you tell me a bit about yourself?

Alternative and related questions:

- Can you talk me through your CV?

The meaning behind the question:
This is, of course, an extremely popular question – and is just the kind an interviewer might throw at you at the beginning of an interview so as to get the ball rolling. They are quite simply placing you centre stage and hoping you will open up to them. Alternatively, they are hopelessly overworked, haven't yet had time to read your CV – and asking you this question will buy them some breathing space!

Your answer:
This is a very broad question – and you might consequently be at a loss as to the approach you should take to answering it.

They are not asking for an autobiography. Focus on discussing major selling points that feature on your CV or application form – selling points that are directly relevant to the job for which you are applying. Don't start telling your whole life history.

While they do want you to open up and paint a picture of yourself, you're not on the psychiatrist's couch here! Keep it professional and avoid getting too personal.

Besides talking about your career, make sure that you have something to say about your education and qualifications – and even your hobbies and interests.

It's vital to practise your answer for this in advance – and try to limit your answer to one minute. If you can't successfully 'pitch' yourself in under a minute then you're going to risk losing the interviewer's attention.

How have you described yourself in the 'Professional Profile' at the top of your CV? A lot of this material can be recycled to help you draft your answer to this question.

> Example:
> I'm a highly driven individual with extensive management experience acquired principally in the aviation sector. Following completion of my degree in International Business (which included a couple of years in Germany) I started my career in administration and have worked my way up to become an Export Sales Manager. I believe I combine a high level of commercial awareness with a commitment to customer care – which helps me to achieve profitable growth in a competitive market. I enjoy being part of, as well as managing, motivating, training and developing, a successful and productive team and I thrive in highly pressurised and challenging working environments. I have strong IT skills, I'm fluent in German and I'm also a qualified First Aider. In my spare time I undertake a wide range of activities; I'm particularly keen on squash and I am also currently working towards my Private Pilot Licence.

2 *Why have you applied for this vacancy?*

Alternative and related questions:

- Why do you want this vacancy?
- What attracted you to this vacancy?
- Why do you think you're suitable for this job?

- What is it that you are looking for in a new job?

The meaning behind the question:
The interviewer is probing to see:

- If you fully understand what the job entails
- How well you might match their requirements
- What appeals to you most about the job

Your answer:
This is another very open-ended question where you might be tempted to say too much. By taking the time to think through your answer to this question in advance, you will be able to remain focused on a few key points.

Your emphasis should be on demonstrating to the interviewer precisely how you match their requirements – and, in doing so, to demonstrate that you fully understand what the role entails.

If you've done your research properly (please see Chapter 1, 'Researching the job') then you will have a good idea of what it is the company is most looking for.

Yes, you have been asked what your motivations are in applying for the vacancy, but try to turn the question round so that the answer you give tells why you are the right candidate for the vacancy.

> Example:
> I've applied for this vacancy because it's an excellent match for my skills and experience – and because it represents a challenge which I know I'll relish. I clearly already have extensive experience as a Senior Quantity Surveyor, including previous experience of rail and station projects – an area I'm particularly interested in. I enjoy managing multiple projects simultaneously. I also enjoy overseeing and coaching junior and assistant quantity surveyors. I'm used to dealing directly with clients; developing productive working relationships with clients is definitely one of my strengths. This role is exactly the sort of role I am currently targeting and I am confident I will be able to make a major contribution.

3 *Why do you wish to leave your current position?*

Alternative and related questions:

- Why do you wish to leave your current employer?
- What do you plan to say to your current employer in your letter of resignation?

The meaning behind the question:
The interviewer is trying to understand your motivation for changing jobs. They clearly want to know why you want to change jobs but they also want to know how serious you are about changing jobs. Are you really committed to moving or are you just wasting their time?

Your answer:
There are a multitude of reasons for wanting to leave your job – but they won't all be positive selling points for you.

Positive reasons include:

- wanting a greater challenge
- wanting to diversify
- seeking greater opportunities
- seeking further advancement
- taking a step up the career ladder.

Negative reasons include:

- problems with your boss
- problems with a colleague
- a financially unstable organisation
- 'personal reasons'.

If your reason for wanting to leave your job is a positive one then your answer will be easy enough to construct. Explain to the interviewer what your motivations are and how the move to your next job will help you to achieve your goals. You are making a positive move for positive reasons and intend to achieve a positive outcome – simple as that.

If, however, your reason for leaving your job is in my list of negative reasons, then giving the right answer is going to be somewhat trickier. Because each of the situations is so different, I will deal with each of them in turn.

Problems with your boss: having problems with the boss is the top reason people give (in surveys) for changing jobs. However, you should never say anything negative about either a current or a previous employer. It isn't professional, it doesn't portray you as someone who is particularly loyal – and it will reflect badly on you. In almost all cases, I would recommend that you avoid citing this as a reason. Criticising your current employer is considered one of the top mistakes you can make at interview and will most likely cost you the job regardless of whether or not your criticism is justified. Aim to give an answer that focuses on the benefits you will experience in moving to your new job rather than making any reference to your having had problems with your boss.

BLOOPER!

Having delivered a particularly devastating critique of his current employer, one candidate was rather shocked to discover that his current employer was in fact the interviewer's brother-in-law!

Problems with a colleague: maybe you want to leave because of a persistently unpleasant colleague? However, explaining this to the interviewer will most likely open you up to expressing bitterness or recrimination – traits that are not attractive to a potential employer. Again, you should aim to give an answer that focuses on the benefits of moving to your new job rather than drawing attention to your problems.

A financially unstable organisation: you may well have decided to leave your job before your employer finally goes bankrupt, but you don't want to be labelled as a 'rat leaving a sinking ship'. It doesn't say much for your loyalty. Avoid giving this as a reason.

'Personal reasons': there are many different personal circumstances that might cause you to wish to leave a job – for example you might simply want a better work–life balance. However, if possible you should avoiding giving 'personal reasons' as an answer and instead leave the interviewer to believe you are leaving in order to pursue a more promising opportunity.

As for asking what you would write in a resignation letter, you should remember that, when it comes to resignation letters, it is well worth being as nice as possible about the matter. Harsh words in a letter of resignation could easily come back to haunt you in the future – not least if you ever need a reference from this employer.

Example:
I would simply tell them that, after careful consideration, I have made the decision to move on to a new challenge. Naturally, I'd thank them for the opportunities with which they presented me during the course of my employment, reassure them that I will of course do my best to help ensure the seamless transfer of my duties and responsibilities before leaving – and wish them all the very best for the future.

4 *Why do you want to work for this organisation?*

Alternative and related questions:

- What is it about our organisation that attracts you?

The meaning behind the question:
The interviewer is analysing your motivations and probing your expectations of the organisation. Why do you want to work for this one in particular? While this question doesn't directly ask what you know about their organisation, in order to be able to answer it effectively you are clearly going to have to demonstrate that you have done your homework.

Your answer:
If you have done your research properly (please see Chapter 2, 'Researching the organisation') you will already be fairly well informed as to the organisation you are applying to join. However, the key to answering this question is how to communicate that knowledge to the interviewer while tying it in with why you want to work for them.

Your focus should be on what in particular attracts you to the organisation. We'll cover the closely related but more generalised question, 'What do you know about us as an organisation?' in the next chapter.

> Example:
> I'm particularly attracted by how progressive an organisation you are. I've seen how your sales levels have grown the past few years and I'm aware of your plans to expand into the United States. Yours is an organisation that is rapidly developing and evolving – and that's exactly what I'm looking for. I want to work for an organisation which is forward-thinking and isn't afraid to tackle new challenges.

5 *What are your strengths?*

Alternative and related questions:

- What are you good at?
- What do you consider yourself to be good at?

The meaning behind the question:
With this question the interviewer wants to achieve the following:

- Identify what your key selling points are.
- Establish whether or not these strengths are relevant to the role they are interviewing for.
- Gain some insight into your character – how self-confident (or arrogant!) you are.

Your answer:
Everyone has their strengths. The key to answering this question is not to rattle off a long list of what you consider your strengths to be. Instead you should be looking to highlight a smaller number of specific strengths,

discussing each one briefly and, most importantly, identifying how these strengths relate to the requirements of the job you are applying to undertake. You can even elaborate on one of your strengths by mentioning a specific relevant achievement.

Choose your strengths carefully. It can be hard to say anything very interesting, for example, about the fact that you are very meticulous and pay great attention to detail. However, if the recruiter is looking for someone to lead a team then you can mention team leadership as one of your strengths – and cite an appropriate example or achievement.

> Example:
> I believe my key strength is that I combine experience of traditional film production with extensive experience in the online arena. I'm very aware of current trends in new media and am able to demonstrate excellent creative judgement. I'm also very good at juggling multiple projects simultaneously; in my current role I frequently have as many as half a dozen different projects on the go at any one time – and I'm committed to completing them all on time and on budget. This clearly requires extremely strong project management skills.

Word of warning:
If you don't give the interviewer at least one specific example to back up your statement then be prepared for them to ask you for one!

6 *What are your weaknesses?*

Alternative and related questions:

- What are you not good at doing?
- What do you find difficult to do and why?
- In what areas do you feel you need to improve?

The meaning behind the question:
With questions of this kind the interviewer wants to achieve the following:

- Identify any weakness which might actually be detrimental to your ability to undertake the role.
- See how you react when faced with a somewhat tricky question.
- Assess how self-aware you are and how you define weakness.

Your answer:
Some might consider this to qualify as a tough interview question and think it should be in a later chapter (Chapter 21, 'The top 25 tough questions: taking the heat'). But believe me – there are much tougher

questions than this! I would only classify this question as 'tricky' rather than tough. While it is superficially a somewhat negative question, it is in fact full of opportunities for you to turn it around to your advantage and make your answer a positive point.

Don't be perturbed by the question or let it throw you off balance. Your answer should be right on the tip of your tongue – because we will work on it right now. And can I just get straight that you should only ever discuss a 'professional' weakness, unless the interviewer specifically requests otherwise (unlikely).

Your first thought might be that you are tempted to say quite simply, 'I don't really have any particular weaknesses.' But this is definitely not the answer the interviewer is looking for – and is definitely not the answer you should be giving.

BLOOPER!

Telling the interviewer your weakness is 'kryptonite' – as one candidate did – is unlikely to amuse an interviewer.

The interviewer wants to know that you are able to look at yourself objectively and to criticise yourself where appropriate. If you honestly don't think you have any weaknesses then you risk coming across as arrogant if you say so – and nobody wants a perfect candidate anyway.

Clearly you don't just want to come up with a straightforward list of what you consider your weaknesses to be. You basically have two choices:

- Talk about a weakness that's not necessarily a weakness at all.
- Talk about a weakness that you turned (or can turn) into a strength.

The problem with the first option is that you risk running into serious cliché territory. I'm talking about the kind of people who answer:

I would have to say that my main weakness is that I'm a perfectionist.

I have a reputation for working too hard; I often push myself far too hard in my work.

You risk sounding as though you plucked your answer straight out of a 1990s manual on interview technique!

Personally, I prefer the second option: talking about a weakness that you turned (or are turning) into a strength.

You are answering the interviewer's question by highlighting a definite weakness but you then go on to reflect positively on this by outlining the active steps you are taking to overcome it. You are demonstrating a willingness to learn, adapt and improve, and you are showing that you have the initiative required to make changes where changes are due.

Choosing a weakness that has its root in lack of experience and therefore has been (or is being) overcome by further training is ideal – because it is a weakness that is relatively easily resolved.

> Example:
> When I first started my current job my first few months were an uphill battle dealing with a backlog of work I inherited from my predecessor. I recognised that I have a weakness when it comes to time management. I have since been on a time management course, read a couple of books on the subject and I believe I've made a lot of progress. But it's something I'm still very vigilant about. I make a concerted effort to apply the principles I've learned every day and to put in place procedures which enable me to most effectively prioritise and process my workload.

This is a good and comprehensive answer meeting all of the objectives we've outlined above.

Word of warning:
Do be prepared for the interviewer to ask the follow-up question, 'OK. That's one weakness. You must surely have more than one weakness?' We'll cover this question in Chapter 21, 'The top 25 tough questions: taking the heat'.

7 What has been your greatest achievement/ accomplishment?

Alternative and related questions:

- What are your biggest achievements?
- What are you most proud of?
- What was your biggest achievement in your current/last job?
- What has been the high point of your career so far?

The meaning behind the question:
Unless the question is qualified by specifically mentioning, for example, your last job, it is important to remember that the interviewer isn't necessarily looking for a work-related achievement. They are looking for evidence of achievement, full stop. However, a work-related achievement is normally what they will be expecting.

Your answer:
You'll want to make sure that you have thought through this question carefully before the interview and have selected both a key professional achievement as well as a key personal achievement: cover both bases.

Try not to go too far back; try to pick a recent achievement. If you've included an 'Achievements' section in your CV (which I would recommend you do) then this will be a good starting point for you to generate ideas.

Describe clearly to the interviewer:

- What it is that you achieved
- What the background and circumstances were
- What impact it had on your career/life

What was the benefit? Try to phrase this in such a way for it to be self-evident that this would also be a benefit to any prospective employer.

> Example:
> My greatest achievement so far in my career would probably be winning the Manager of the Year award last year. I made numerous operational changes at my branch, including a massive reduction in stock levels – which significantly boosted our working capital. I also drove up sales levels, especially by increasing the uptake of after-sales insurance packages. The net effect was that we smashed the previous branch sales record by an impressive 37 per cent - and profits rose in line with this. This directly resulted in my promotion to the management of the flagship Edinburgh branch.

8 What can you, above all the other applicants, bring to this job?

Alternative and related questions:

- What makes you the best candidate for this job?

The meaning behind the question:
The interviewer is directly asking you what your 'unique selling point' is. They are looking for at least one significant reason that you should be their no. 1 choice for the job.

Your answer:
Well, what does make you the best candidate for this job?

I'll level with you – this isn't necessarily a top ten question in terms of how likely you are to get asked it. However, it is very much a top ten question in terms of the importance of your having prepared an answer to it. You need to go into each and every interview with a thorough understanding of what it is that you have to offer. If you don't know what it is that you're offering then how can you hope to be able to sell it effectively?

If you do get asked this specific question then don't be afraid to answer it quite candidly. It's a bold question and warrants a bold answer. The interviewer is really putting you on the spot to sell yourself. But do be very careful to avoid coming across as arrogant – because that's the last thing you want to do. It's a fine line you need to tread.

Feel free to cite an example from your past where you demonstrated that you are someone who is capable of going the extra mile. It's all very well to say that you're someone who gives 110 per cent (although it is a bit of a cliché) but if you can actually throw an example at your interviewer then you're going to be a whole lot more credible.

BLOOPER!

One ex-army candidate for a management role replied, 'I can shoot someone at 300 yards.' What is more amazing is that he actually got the job! This is a rare example of a sense of humour working to the candidate's advantage.

Example:
Having now been working in this industry for over a decade, I have developed successful relationships with key decision-makers in numerous companies, enabling me to achieve a sales conversion rate much higher than average. This is undoubtedly a very challenging role, requiring considerable drive and determination, but I believe my previous sales record is clear evidence that I am more than capable of achieving what it is that you need.

9 Where do you see yourself in five years' time?

Alternative and related questions:

- How long do you plan to stay/would you stay in this job if we offer it to you?
- What are your long-term career goals?
- How does this job fit into your long-term career plans?
- How far do you feel you might rise in our organisation?

The meaning behind the question:
The interviewer is trying to ascertain what your long-term career ambitions are. They want to get a better understanding of your motivations.

They will normally be looking for someone who is keen to learn, develop and progress. However, they are recruiting for a specific role and will want someone who is prepared to commit to that role for a reasonable period of time.

You may think this question is just a cliché and doesn't really get asked in practice. Trust me – it does – and far more frequently than you might imagine.

Your answer:
Yes, lots of people will think they're displaying a great sense of humour/ambition/self-confidence to reply, 'Doing your job!' I wouldn't recommend it though – because it will all too easily come across as arrogant and aggressive.

Avoid being too specific. It's very difficult for most people to know exactly what job they will be undertaking in five years' time and so it can come across as unrealistic to quote a specific job title you are aiming for. Try to present your answer more in terms of what level you hope you will have reached – what level of responsibility, of autonomy. It's also a good idea if you can phrase your answer to communicate that you hope you will still be with this same organisation in five years' time.

> Example:
> Five years from now I expect I will have progressed significantly in my career and be making an even greater contribution. Having proved my value to the organisation I would hope to have been given increased responsibilities and greater challenges. I've clearly given a good deal of thought to working for you and I can see that there are indeed a lot of opportunities both for promotion and for ongoing professional development. My career is very important to me and I want to push myself hard to deliver the very best of which I'm capable.

10 You've mentioned x under the 'Interests and Activities' on your CV. Can you tell me a bit more about that?

Alternative and related questions:

- What activities do you enjoy outside of work?
- What are you interested in outside of work?

The meaning behind the question:
There are a variety of possible reasons interviewers might ask this question:

- They're trying to get some insight into your personality and character.
- They're testing to see how truthful you've been on your CV.
- They've run out of other questions and are killing time!

Besides knowing whether you're capable of actually doing the job, most employers are keen to know what sort of a person you would be like to work alongside. Employers are generally keen to have a diversity of characters within their team and are always on the lookout for someone who can add a new dimension to the team.

While nobody has yet conducted a survey specifically to research this, there is plenty of anecdotal evidence of recruiters deciding to call someone in for an interview purely as a result of what they have included in their CV under 'Interests and Activities'. I, for one, will admit to having done so when hiring.

Your answer:
This is a very simple question to answer – provided, as always, that you've prepared for it in advance. If you have a hobby that makes for an interesting talking point at the interview then it will reflect positively on you as an individual.

You should of course be able to back up anything you've listed on your CV. If you mention chess to give your CV some intellectual clout, but haven't actually played since you were at school, then you could well come a cropper in your interview if your interviewer turns out to be a chess fan and asks you which openings to the game you favour!

It's always a good idea if you can subtly slip in mention of any positions of responsibility you hold outside of work. If your passion is, for example, football, and you're also the captain of the local team, then do say so.

Besides the obvious selling point of football being a team activity (and hence your being a 'team player'), you've immediately communicated your leadership qualities, your ability to take responsibility for others, your ability to commit yourself to a project, etc.

Example:
I've always been fascinated by planes. I remember my first flight as a child; it was a thrilling experience. Even though I understand the science behind it, I'm still in awe each and every time I see a plane clear the runway. It's quite an expensive hobby to pursue but, as soon as I could afford to do so, I started taking flying lessons. I gained my Private Pilot Licence, went on to qualify as an Instructor and I'm now a senior member of my local flying club. While it's not something I've ever wished to pursue as a career, I do enjoy giving the occasional lesson and generally participating in the club community. It's definitely something about which I'm very passionate.

Chapter 20

Fifty more classic questions: be prepared

There are many interview question books which feature hundreds of different questions and answers. While you might have time to quickly read through them, you're unlikely to have the time – or the inclination – to look at any of them in any great depth, nor to think through your own answers to the questions.

If you look closely at all these hundreds of questions, you'll see that many of them are simply variations on a theme and that the same core themes come up again and again. There are so many different ways to word a question but only a limited number of topics the interviewer is likely to be interested in.

I believe that rather than spoon-feeding you the answers to hundreds of questions it's much more important for you to recognise and fully understand the different lines of questioning an interviewer is likely to take. Within each individual theme there will be a cluster of closely related questions all attempting to address the same issue.

I have condensed hundreds of interview questions down to a list of 50 questions which cover pretty much every key issue an interviewer is likely to tackle you on. We'll be looking at these in detail in this chapter.

So-called 'tough' questions

Many questions which you might, at first sight, consider to be 'tough' are actually nothing more than alternatively – and more aggressively – phrased versions of classic questions.

For example, instead of asking you the relatively innocuous question, 'How far do you feel you might rise in our organisation?' your interviewer – if they are the sadistic sort – might ask you, 'Would you like to have my job?'

Clearly there will be differences in how you respond to each of these questions but the core answer is the same.

I'm not saying that tough questions don't exist; they most certainly do (and we'll be covering them in the next chapter). But most of the questions you're likely to encounter, which might traditionally be seen as tough, really aren't that tough at all once you've understood what it is the interviewer is driving at. If you can see through to the meaning behind the question then it can take a lot of the sting out of a question.

1 How would you describe yourself? / How would your boss/colleagues/team/family/friends describe you?

Alternative and related questions:

- What do you think your references will say about you?
- What kind of person are you to work with?

The meaning behind the question:
The interviewer wants to assess how you perceive yourself. Whether they ask how you would describe yourself or how others would describe you, the question is all about your perception of yourself – seeing yourself as others see you.

Your answer:
This is a very popular question and could conceivably have made my top ten. It's vital to be prepared for it.

You will want to make sure that you have a few well-chosen adjectives up your sleeve ready to answer this question, e.g. loyal, dedicated, ambitious, determined, independent, highly motivated, understanding, etc. Tell the interviewer what they want to hear! But don't be too big-headed; a little modesty can go a long way.

It's a difficult balance to strike but I hope the following example will show you how to achieve this.

> Example:
> I would describe myself as a very determined and highly motivated person. I do take my job seriously but I'm able to see things in perspective and believe I'm quite easy-going to work with. I'm an optimist rather than a pessimist – but I'm also a realist and I cope well when the going gets tough; I'm very good at finding solutions to problems. Above all, I would say I'm a positive and enthusiastic person – and I relish a challenge.

Word of warning:
There's no need to back up this answer with examples – such as outlining a time when you were particularly understanding with a colleague. It would be going too far.

2 In what ways are you a team player?

Alternative and related questions:

- Do you prefer working on your own or as part of a team?
- How would you define teamwork?

- ➢ Can you tell me about a team you worked in and the role you played within that team?
- ➢ What do you think makes a perfect team?

The meaning behind the question:
Teamwork is essential in almost any work environment. Questioning your ability to work in a team is therefore one of an interviewer's favourites. They will be looking for evidence of a number of core abilities:

- ➢ The ability to communicate effectively with others.
- ➢ The ability to recognise and understand the viewpoints of others.
- ➢ The ability to appreciate the contribution you are expected to make.

Your answer:
This is a very important and popular question, which could be phrased in many different ways. As well as pre-preparing your answer to 'In what ways are you a team player', you should also draft answers to all the alternative questions I've listed above. There will be common ground between your answers but each will have a slightly different slant to it.

You could answer the question in the context of your current job but you'd be better off approaching it from the angle of the job for which you are applying. You're being asked in what ways you are a team player but you need to be asking yourself in what ways will they want you to be a team player. Are they looking for a leader? Are they looking for someone who brings out the best in others? Are they looking for the person who generates the ideas or the person who is a dab hand at putting new ideas into practice?

Establish in your own mind what sort of a team player they want you to be and then deliver an answer which caters to that image.

> Example:
> I certainly very much enjoy working with others; I'm outgoing, I enjoy the team spirit and I'm understanding of the needs of others. I'm good at helping members of the team to see the bigger picture – to see the wood from the trees – helping them to focus on what really matters rather than getting bogged down in irrelevant detail. I'm also good at helping the team to spot flaws in our approach – and potential problems and pitfalls. I believe I have strong communication skills and, while I don't yet have experience in a leadership role, I do have a talent for liaising between different team members and resolving any disputes which may arise. Conflict between different team members is rarely very productive and is normally best avoided.

3 *Do you work well on your own initiative?*

Alternative and related questions:

- Are you able to manage your own workload?

The meaning behind the question:
Given the choice between someone who can be left to get on with a job and someone who needs constant supervision, who would you hire?

Employees who work well on their own initiative are highly prized.

With this question, the interviewer is purely seeking evidence that you are such an employee.

Your answer:
Of course you work well on your own initiative. But how can you prove that to the interviewer? This is a 'closed' question but it certainly requires more than a one-word answer. It's a great chance for you to roll out a pre-prepared example, which ticks all the interviewer's boxes and shows you in a positive light.

If the interviewer is asking you this question, the chances are that in the role you're applying for you will be expected to be able to work on your own initiative. If you've studied the job description carefully you should be able to identify under what circumstances this will be required. Choosing an example from a past (or present) job, which closely matches these circumstances, is naturally going to have a much stronger impact.

> Example:
> I enjoy working with others but I'm equally able to work on my own initiative. I'm not afraid to ask for guidance if necessary but I'm quick to learn and, once I've understood what's required of me, I am more than capable of getting on with the job under my own steam. In my current role I work as part of a close-knit team but that's not to say that there aren't certain tasks and projects I have to handle on my own. For example, I have sole responsibility for reconciling credits and debits on our bank statements to our sales and purchase ledgers. It's not a task that can be shared with anyone; it's not a two-man job. I set aside one day a week to concentrate on this – because it does require a lot of concentration – reconciling entries which match and taking steps to resolve any discrepancies.

Word of warning:
Even if you do prefer to work on your own, it's best not to mention this. You don't want to risk being labelled 'not a team player'. This question doesn't ask whether you prefer to work on your own; it simply asks how capable you are of doing so.

4 *What techniques do you use to get things done?*

Alternative and related questions:

➢ How do you get things done at work?

The meaning behind the question:
This is a very simple question. The interviewer wants to know what your working style is – how do you plan and organise yourself to ensure that you achieve your objectives? They do just want to hear you say that you're a very organised and efficient person – they want proof of exactly how you get things done.

Your answer:
Tell it like it is. The interviewer isn't expecting any magic tricks or a treatise on the latest management techniques. Your answer just needs to outline the systems and tools you use to manage your workload so as to ensure that everything which needs to get done does get done. You should aim to place emphasis on this last point – that the techniques you use are ones that clearly work for you.

> Example:
> Careful planning is critical to my ability to get things done: planning, organisation and action. I rely heavily on 'to-do' lists. These enable me to capture and record everything which I need to action. I maintain a master to-do list but also have separate to-do lists for each particular project I'm handling. I review these at least once a day so as to identify my priorities. I always aim to focus on tasks that have deadlines attached to them and also tasks which will achieve the most in the shortest space of time. Less important items I will either postpone, delegate or, if I am unable to clearly identify the benefits, remove from the list completely. Whilst I have a very heavy workload to juggle, I find that these systems enable me to always keep one step ahead and ensure that nothing slips through the net.

5 *What motivates you?*

Alternative and related questions:

➢ What do you need to retain your motivation?

The meaning behind the question:
What the interviewer is really asking is, 'What would we have to do to motivate you?' and, 'Would you be sufficiently motivated to undertake this job effectively?' They are unlikely to ask this directly, though. By asking you the more open-ended 'What motivates you?' they are likely to extract a lot more

useful information out of you – if you are careless enough to let it slip! Interviewers want to hire highly motivated people – not people who are just going to go through the motions until it's time to go home.

Your answer:
There are lots of different things which could motivate you. You've got to be careful to pick factors:

- which will reflect positively on you as an individual
- which are not inconsistent with the job for which you are applying
- which are equally of benefit to your prospective employer
- which will not impose any kind of a burden on the employer.

I'm not going to hide the fact that money is of course a major motivator. It's the primary reason most people go to work each day! However, unless you are in sales or some other highly money-driven and largely commission-based role then you should steer clear of mentioning money as a motivating factor. It's too selfish an answer. It's a factor that is purely in your own interests and not your prospective employer's.

I would recommend that, depending on the nature of your role, you cite factors such as challenges, results and recognition – and elaborate on these so as to demonstrate their value to your employer.

> Example:
> I'm very results-driven. Doing a good job and achieving the desired end result is my primary motivation. While I enjoy working on a project on my own, I'm particularly motivated by the buzz of working in a team. It's very rewarding working closely with others who share the same common goal. I like to take on a challenge; I like to rise to that challenge as part of a concerted team effort – and I naturally appreciate it when my boss compliments me on a job well done.

6 Are you proactive?

Alternative and related questions:

- How good are you at taking the initiative?

The meaning behind the question:
Being proactive means making an effort to anticipate a situation and acting in advance either to prepare for it or to prevent it. It's not exactly the same as taking the initiative but the two are certainly closely related.

In asking you this question, the interviewer wants to establish what your definition of proactive is and whether or not you are indeed proactive yourself – because it is a highly desirable characteristic.

Your answer:
This is a prime example of a question requiring you to deliver a specific example – whether or not the interviewer actually asks you for one. If you fail to illustrate your answer with an example then it's going to be fairly meaningless. Anyone can claim to be proactive, but can you actually prove it?

Choose your example carefully in advance, describe the circumstances to the interviewer and, most importantly, explain what the benefits of your actions were.

> Example:
> Yes, I would consider myself to be proactive. I believe it's very important to be as proactive as possible. As the saying goes, a stitch in time saves nine! When my team is working on a project I always do my best to identify possible problems in advance and to make sure that we address them. Recently, a major project of ours was severely affected by a key member of staff leaving the company overnight (for personal reasons). I anticipated that, as a result of this, we wouldn't be able to deliver the solution to the client on time. I took the decision to contact the client, explain the situation, apologise for the delay but make the point that the quality of the finished solution was of greater importance than delivering it on schedule. The client appreciated my honesty, was very understanding and was pleased to hear that we'd never compromise on quality just to be seen to meet a deadline.

7 Are you creative?

Alternative and related questions:

- In what ways would you say you were creative?
- Are you innovative/inventive?

The meaning behind the question:
There's no hidden meaning here. It's a very direct question; every walk of life requires at least some degree of creativity – and creativity is often seen as an indicator of intelligence. My core question, 'Are you creative?', is clearly a closed question, but answering it with a straight 'Yes' isn't going to get you anywhere. Regardless of precisely how the interviewer phrases the question you need to aim to say precisely in what ways you are creative, how this applies to your line of work – and to back this up with at least one example.

Your answer:
Some lines of work are clearly more creative than others and the way you phrase your answer will naturally depend on exactly what it is that you do for a living. If you work in a creative field then clearly you will need to give

a much more comprehensive answer. But even if you work in a field that isn't generally seen as particularly demanding in terms of creativity you should be able to come up with an example of where you have displayed lateral or 'outside-the-box' thinking or invented a new and better way of handling something.

Example:
Yes, I believe I'm a creative individual. I'm certainly able to think laterally and to be inventive in terms of finding solutions to problems. Quantity surveying isn't generally seen as a particularly creative profession but I have nevertheless used my creative abilities on numerous occasions, for example converting old manual systems of reporting to highly automated – and much more accurate – spreadsheet-based systems. This saved myself and my team a considerable amount of time in the long term as well as meaning we were less exposed to the professional embarrassment of errors in our calculations.

8 Are you a risk-taker?

Alternative and related questions:

- How do you feel about taking risks?
- Do you have a problem with taking risks?

The meaning behind the question:
'Are you a risk-taker?' is a very direct question. What the interviewer is really looking for is to assess what your *attitude* is to taking risks. In some lines of work someone who takes risks is definitely going to be a liability. However, in many lines of work the ability to weigh up risks – and to take *calculated* risks – is an important skill.

Your answer:
Your answer will inevitably depend on exactly what the job is that you are applying for. If your line of work is one in which taking risks – or cutting corners – is likely to be frowned upon, then you're going to need to formulate your answer so as to make it clear that you are not someone who believes in risks. You may even want to emphasise that you see it as part of your job to identify potential risks and pre-empt them.

If assessing risks – and taking appropriate risks – is going to be a feature of your new job then your answer will naturally be very different. You certainly want to avoid the impression of being in any way reckless, though. Your emphasis should be on the steps you take to identify and gauge risks, only taking risks where you have calculated the potential outcomes and deemed that your actions are going to be worth the risk. You should also make some mention of your decision-making capabilities, because being prepared to take calculated risks is, ultimately, a form of decision-making.

Example:
It depends on how you define risk. I am certainly not somebody who takes unnecessary risks, nor risks that would in any way compromise anyone's personal safety. However, I fully appreciate that commercial success is dependent on taking risks – calculated risks. If, having given a matter careful consideration and weighed up the possible ramifications, I determine that a risk is – in the best interests of the business – worth taking, then I am not afraid to take it. You can't always be right – but careful planning and analysis should tip the odds in your favour and ensure that, overall, your decisions pay off. Experience is, of course, essential – and the experience I have gained over the course of my career is invaluable in informing my decisions.

9 How do you handle pressure and stress?

Alternative and related questions:

- Can you tell me about a time when you were under significant pressure and how you handled that?
- Do you thrive under pressure?
- How do you cope with the numerous conflicting demands on your time?
- What causes you stress at work and why?

The meaning behind the question:
The ability to cope with pressure and stress is essential in almost all walks of life, whether you're working on the checkout at the supermarket or heading up a major corporation. Pressure and stress are unavoidable aspects of the world we live in. The interviewer will be looking to identify:

- That you recognise that pressure and stress are facts of life
- That you understand the effect pressure and stress has on you
- That you are sufficiently robust to be able to take them in your stride.

Your answer:
Because of the variety of ways in which an interviewer can question you on this topic, it's important that you fully understand what the difference is between pressure and stress – because many people use the two terms interchangeably.

Being under pressure is a matter of having significant demands made of you – being challenged to achieve something that is either difficult to achieve in and of itself, or difficult to achieve within the time frame that has been set. Pressure is largely a positive force and a motivating factor for many people.

Stress, on the other hand, is not so positive. Stress occurs when the pressure you are under exceeds your ability to effectively meet the demands being made of you. Stress is essentially what an individual experiences when exposed to excessive pressure – and long-term stress can cause all sorts of problems.

I am sure that everyone reading this book will, at some stage in their lives, have experienced pressure and stress, and know exactly what it's like.

The key to formulating your answer to this question is to seize this as an opportunity to talk about a situation or an occasion where you were under pressure – and how you rose to the challenge. Try to avoid talking about an occasion when you were totally stressed out – but do acknowledge that you understand stress and are able to deal with it appropriately.

Avoid conveying the impression that the fact you were under pressure was in any way your own fault – or due to your own personal failings. Place the 'blame' firmly on external factors outside of your control.

Different lines of work are of course subject to different levels of pressure and stress and this will have a bearing on how precisely you phrase your answer.

> Example:
> Working for a small start-up company the past few years has naturally been quite a high-pressure experience on occasion. I've had to deal with numerous conflicting demands on my time – and often very limited resources. With careful planning and organisation you can normally reduce the pressure you are under – but there will always be factors at play which are outside of your control. Personally, while it makes a nice break to have a few pressure-free days, I generally thrive under pressure. I use it to help channel my energies into accomplishing as much as possible. Naturally, there are sometimes occasions when the pressure I'm put under is excessive and this can be stressful. However, I'm sufficiently experienced to appreciate that there is only so much you can reasonably be expected to be capable of and the solution is not to panic but to remain focused on delivering your very best.

10 Can you tell me about a time when you have failed to achieve a goal?

Alternative and related questions:

- What's the biggest failure you've experienced in your career?
- Can you tell me about a time when you've failed to meet an important deadline?

The meaning behind the question:
As well as pinpointing a particular 'failure' in your career, the interviewer will also be gauging your overall attitude to failure – how you deal with adversity. Everyone experiences some failures during the course of their careers but not everybody bounces back and learns as much from the experience as they perhaps should.

Your answer:
You might think this is a tough question because there's no way to answer it without admitting failure. But it's not really that tough. The secret is to avoid picking too major a failure and, whatever example you choose, to subtly blame the failure on factors outside of your control. You should be very wary indeed of laying the blame at the doorstep of a former boss or colleague; this can backfire on you spectacularly. However, you can certainly dilute some of the blame by saying that you were working 'as part of a team' at the time.

> Example:
> In my last job we were given the opportunity to pitch for a major contract – at relatively short notice. I was part of a team that spent a good couple of weeks working very hard on the tender and it was clear that our company was undoubtedly the best choice for the contract. Unfortunately, the client had employed a rather inexperienced individual to review the tenders and they fell for a competitor's sales pitch – which had a lot less substance but a lot more spin. It was a major blow. I was naturally very disappointed at what seemed a very unfair decision, especially having put so much effort into the tender – but I put it down to experience and got on with successfully bidding for other contracts. The following year, the client having been very dissatisfied with our competitor's performance, we were asked to re-tender for the contract. This time, we won it. We did of course learn some lessons from our previous failure but, most of all, we were fortunate that the individual responsible for reviewing the tenders this time was a lot more experienced.

Word of warning:
Don't be tempted to say you've never failed. The interviewer won't believe you!

11 *What's the worst mistake you've made at work and how did you deal with it?*

Alternative and related questions:

- Can you tell me about a time when you made a major error at work?

The meaning behind the question:
What the interviewer is trying to extract from you here is not an admission of guilt but a demonstration of how you reacted to your error and what steps you took to resolve it. You can learn a lot about someone from the way they handle mistakes.

Your answer:
As with the previous question, you might think this is rather a tough one. The interviewer has specifically asked you about the very worst mistake you've ever made at work. The key is to realise that everyone makes mistakes; the important thing is to learn from them and make sure you never make the same mistake twice.

Also, just because they've asked you what the worst mistake you've made was, that doesn't necessarily mean you have to tell them! Try to talk about a mistake that was clearly severe but one that is unlikely to put them off hiring you completely. How? By choosing carefully and placing the emphasis on what you did to resolve the situation – and what you learned from the experience.

If you can subtly apportion some of the blame to circumstances out of your control – or if you can choose an example that didn't directly involve your work – then it's going to strengthen your answer. It also helps if you can pick an example which goes back some way in time. However, you definitely need to avoid coming across as someone who can't admit their own mistakes.

> Example:
> I think the worst mistake I ever made at work was in my first ever job – five years ago now. A more senior member of the team seemed to take an instant dislike to me from the start – and one day she was particularly unpleasant to me in front of several colleagues. Later on, I was talking to one of those colleagues who was, I thought, attempting to console me. Angry and hurt, I foolishly vented my feelings and told her what I thought of the lady in question. I was naturally shocked to find out that she went on to tell everyone what I

had said and this certainly didn't help my relationship with the team member who was causing me problems. Rather than let the situation carry on, I chose to have a quiet word with this lady so as to find out what her problem was with me and to see if we could put it behind us. It turned out it was nothing personal; she just resented the fact that a friend of hers had also been interviewed for my position and had been turned down. Once we had got matters out into the air, her behaviour changed and we actually got on quite well after that. However, I certainly learned a lot from the experience. I learned that careful communication is vital in managing interpersonal relationships and that if I have a problem with someone it's always best to talk it over with them rather than with someone else.

BLOOPER!

Do choose your example carefully. I once had a candidate tell me about the time she 'lost' a leg. She was working as a runner in an operating theatre and the surgeon handed her the limb he had just amputated. She put it down and, unfortunately, forgot all about it. 'To this day I don't really know what happened to that leg ...', she reminisced wistfully.

12 How would you handle the following situation?

Alternative and related questions:

- What would you do if you were presented with the following scenario?

The meaning behind the question:
Often, an interviewer may pose a hypothetical, scenario-based question, telling you to imagine yourself in a difficult or negative situation and asking how you would deal with it.

By confronting you with an unexpected situation and getting you to think on your feet, they can tell a lot about how you would actually react under such circumstances.

Your answer:
The answer you should give will of course depend on the precise scenario the interviewer outlines. You need to try to identify what the expectations of you would be under the circumstances – and highlight the skills and techniques you would use to deal with the situation.

For the purposes of the example below, please imagine the following scenario: You are a receptionist working on the front desk when all of a sudden a fax arrives, several phone lines start ringing, an important client walks in and a courier turns up with a package that requires your signature. How do you cope with this situation?

In this example, you should be able to identify that the interviewer is probing your ability to prioritise, to 'fire-fight' – and to not panic!

Example:
My first priority would be to answer the calls whilst simultaneously presenting the waiting clients and the courier with a professional and friendly smile. The calls can be answered and either be put straight through or be put on hold, allowing me to deal with the client and then the courier thereafter. The people waiting in front of me are able to see just how busy I am, whereas those on the phone will simply feel ignored if their calls are not answered promptly – and may hang up. Having successfully prioritised the calls and the visitors, I would then be able to respond to the fax when there is more time.

13 *Can you tell me about a major project you have successfully completed?*

Alternative and related questions:

- Can you tell me about a major project that you have recently managed?

The meaning behind the question:
The interviewer isn't really interested in the project itself; they are interested in how you successfully completed the project; looking for evidence of your ability to successfully complete a project and trying to ascertain how your key skills contribute to this ability.

Your answer:
The emphasis in this question is on a project that you have *successfully* completed. It's a perfect opportunity to blow your own trumpet.

Make the very most of this question to highlight your skills and abilities which led to the successful completion of the project – being careful to pick those which are most of relevance to the job for which you are now applying. Make your contribution to the project clear. What role did you have to play in its success?

Unless the interviewer specifically asks you for a project for which you had sole responsibility, it is reasonable to assume that they are happy with you talking about a project you worked on as part of a team – which is the case with the majority of projects.

It is also best to talk about a project you completed recently. If you go too far back, the interviewer might wonder why you can't cite a more recent example.

Example:
I was recently involved in organising our participation at a trade fair. It was a very major project. We'd never done a trade fair before but we felt it could be a useful method of drumming up new business. It took a considerable amount of planning and organisation on my part; I had to assess everything that would need to be arranged in advance, from hiring the lighting set-up to liaising with our designers on the production of appropriate corporate literature for us to hand out. I had to make sure I didn't miss the smallest of details – for example, I had to check the plans of our stand to ensure our extension cables were long enough to reach all our equipment. On the day itself, we were on site very early to make sure everything was in place, tested and fully functioning prior to the arrival of the visitors – just in case there were any last minute hitches, which, thankfully, there weren't. The event was very successful and our stand attracted a lot of attention. It was a very busy day. We were able to pitch our services to hundreds of people and pass on their contact details for our sales team to follow up on. Following the success of this event, we're now looking at future events we can attend.

14 Can you tell me about a major problem at work that you've had to deal with?

Alternative and related questions:

- Can you tell me about a major project you were involved with that went wrong?

The meaning behind the question:
Problems are inevitable, no matter what your line of work. The interviewer isn't particularly interested in the problem per se. What they are interested in is how you dealt with it – what action you took and what the outcome of that action was.

Employers don't want problems; they want solutions – and they rely on their staff to deliver those solutions. The interviewer wants to make sure that you're just the type of employee who would be able to do that.

Your answer:
This isn't the same question as Question 11, 'What's the worst mistake you've made at work and how did you deal with it?', so make sure that you don't give the same answer! It would definitely be a blunder to pick an

example of a problem which you yourself had caused – or indeed which was caused by a colleague of yours.

You should also avoid picking a problem where a colleague or a member of your staff was themself the problem. Try to choose a simpler and less controversial topic. The best examples to pick are those where the problem was caused by circumstances beyond your organisation's control.

Since they're referring to a problem in the past, it's important for you to choose an example which not only highlights your problem-solving capabilities but shows them to be relevant to the job for which you are now applying.

> Example:
> The weather caused us major problems just a couple of months ago. There was very heavy overnight snowfall and, with all the buses cancelled and only a few trains running, only a few members of our admin team managed to get into work. There was nothing for it but to fire-fight – we didn't have enough staff to get everything done that would normally need to be done. I established what our main priorities were – what activities were most essential to the running of our department – and made sure that we had those covered. I identified less important tasks that we could postpone for a few days until we had the full team back. I also spoke to all the missing team members to see if there were any other urgent priorities of which we, in the office, were unaware. We worked hard and fast – right through lunch – and, despite feeling that the phone was always ringing, we managed to keep everything running smoothly until things were back to normal.

15 *We have a problem with x. How would you resolve that?*

Alternative and related questions:

- Can you tell me about a difficult problem that you resolved?
- Can you tell me about a major problem at work that you've had to deal with?

The meaning behind the question:
Following on from the previous question, this question is, again, directly probing your problem-solving capabilities but, more than that, is doing so in a way that is directly relevant to the job for which you are applying.

The interviewer is trying to identify what you could really bring to the organisation.

The interviewer is also assessing how able you are to think on your feet – because they will know there is no way you could have pre-prepared your answer to this one!

Your answer:
Problem 'x' could be just about anything. It could be a hypothetical problem but it's more likely to be a real-life problem currently facing your prospective employer.

The main difficulty you face with this question is, of course, that it's almost impossible to prepare for in advance. You're going to have to think fast. However, rather than replying immediately I'd suggest you buy some time by getting the interviewer to talk a little more about the problem. Don't be afraid to ask a few questions first to make sure that you fully understand what the problem is – and what the circumstances are. As well as arming you with more facts, this will also give you some valuable thinking time.

If you're asked the alternative question, 'Can you tell me about a difficult problem that you resolved?', then you're lucky – because you can prepare a perfect example for this well in advance of the interview. Please refer to the previous question, Question 14, 'Can you tell me about a major problem at work that you've had to deal with?', for details of how best to handle this.

16 What do you do when you disagree with your line manager?

Alternative and related questions:

- What would you do if you disagreed with a decision taken by your line manager?
- Would you make your opinion known if you disagreed with a decision taken by a superior?

The meaning behind the question:
Ostensibly, you might think the interviewer is testing to see how subordinate you are. This isn't really the case though. It's not to an organisation's advantage to be filled with people who never question authority – or who never voice their opinion. What the interviewer is really looking for is to identify the manner in which you would express your disagreement.

Your answer:
A lot depends, of course, on precisely what it is that you disagree with. Is it a minor issue which boils down to a matter of your judgement against theirs – or is it a more serious situation which could potentially call for your having to go 'over their head' and discuss the matter with their superior.

You should avoid talking about the second possibility. Build your answer around the scenario of a minor disagreement and place the emphasis on how you would use your communication and interpersonal skills.

Example:
Inevitably there will be times when I disagree with my manager's point of view – or with a decision she has taken or intends to take. In my current role, my manager welcomes input from her team and, while I appreciate that it isn't appropriate to openly disagree with her, I will query issues in private with her as necessary. There may be factors leading to her decision of which I am unaware. Alternatively, once we've both discussed our thoughts, we may simply agree to disagree. I have to respect that, at the end of the day, it remains her prerogative to make a decision whether I agree with it or not – and to support her in that course of action to the best of my ability.

17 How would you describe yourself as a manager?

Alternative and related questions:

- What is your management style?
- How do you manage people?

The meaning behind the question:
There's nothing too complex about this question. The interviewer wants to know what your perception of leadership is and how you go about the day-to-day responsibility of management.

You're only going to be asked this question if you're applying for a management-level role and the interviewer is hoping to gauge just how successful you are likely to be in fulfilling such a role.

It's also going to be of interest to them to see how you perceive yourself. It can say a lot about you as a person.

Your answer:
Unless you really are the perfect manager, try to interpret this question in terms of the manager you aspire to be – because that's the kind of manager the interviewer is wanting you to be!

There are two main aspects to a management role:

- Getting the job done.
- Handling the people who will help you to get the job done.

Your answer needs to cover both these bases.
The precise points you raise in your answer will depend on the kind of management role for which you are applying. Different employers will have different expectations of how their managers should behave and what they are expected to achieve.

BLOOPER!

'I don't do anything that I can make someone else do for me!'

Example:
I'm a very hands-on manager. While I am clearly in charge of my team, we are nonetheless a team – and I am very much a member of that team. When the circumstances require it, I will assert my authority and lead my staff in the direction I have determined we should go. However, I'm always open to input, ideas and suggestions and consider myself to be very approachable in that respect. I realise the importance of motivating my staff to deliver their best and I'm tactful and diplomatic when dealing with potential problems; I believe a lot more can be achieved through communication than through conflict. I am nevertheless very results-driven and expect every member of my team to pull their weight and help us to achieve our common goals.

18 Can you give me an example of when you have successfully coached a member of your team?

Alternative and related questions:

- Have you ever been asked to help train a new member of staff?

The meaning behind the question:
You'd be wrong in thinking that this is a question just for managers. This question could be asked of anyone who works in a team – which is pretty much everyone! In all lines of work the ability to help others to further develop their skills and experience is a valuable attribute. How you describe your example will tell the interviewer a lot about you.

Your answer:
You need to structure your answer logically so as to identify what the circumstances were, why the individual needed coaching, how you went about coaching them and, most important of all, what the outcome was. Coaching a team member is a project like any other. In order to deliver a successful answer to this question you're going to need to demonstrate a successful outcome to your efforts.

The example you select will depend on your own personal experiences but, whatever example you choose, make sure that you come out of it as the hero of the day.

If you're struggling to find an example then the easiest is normally to pick a time when you had to help deal with a new member of staff. Coaching is a very broad term and helping to train a new colleague certainly falls under its umbrella.

Example:
In my current job for a mail-order company, I work as part of a team, processing orders received and liaising directly with our customers by telephone to handle and resolve any problems or queries. While administration forms the majority of the workload, there's also a lot of customer contact. Recently, my manager took the decision to hire a new team member who had a lot of very valuable customer-facing experience but not so much administrative experience. While the new member of staff clearly needed no help dealing with customers on the telephone, it was obvious from the start that she was struggling with the administrative side of things. As one of the most experienced members of the team, my manager asked if I could take this lady under my wing and help her to resolve the administrative difficulties she was having. Over a period of several days I took the time for her to initially shadow me in the work I was doing, before moving on for me to let her do the work herself under my careful observation. She learned very quickly and within the week she was fully up to scratch and has since become an invaluable member of the team.

19 What is your customer service philosophy?

Alternative and related questions:

- Can you tell me about a difficult client/customer you've had and how you handled them?
- Can you give me an example of an occasion when you exceeded a client's/customer's expectations?

The meaning behind the question:
Most organisations provide a product or service to a customer. Some definitions of 'customer' are obvious: Marks & Spencer sells sandwiches to the public. Some are less obvious: the Job Centre helps the unemployed return to work.

Customer service skills are consequently of importance in many different walks of life – and this question is designed to probe your customer service skills. It is more far-reaching than that, though, because many of the same skills which will enable an individual to work well with customers will also help them to work well with their colleagues.

Your answer:
However the interviewer phrases the question, the main thrust of your answer should be to outline your customer service skills.

If you can illustrate your answer with an example of when you have delivered outstanding customer service, then so much the better. Outstanding customer service could include resolving a difficult client's complaint or it could be a case of your having exceeded a customer's expectations. Whatever example you select, make sure it is one which shows you in a positive light, i.e. if you want to talk about a dissatisfied client then it had better not be your actions which caused the dissatisfaction!

> Example:
> I believe the customer is central to everything we do. Profits are certainly our ultimate goal but, without customer satisfaction, profits will suffer. I consequently attach a lot of importance to customer service. A business is nothing without its customers and it's vital to recognise this. I believe I have strong customer service skills – and working with the public is certainly something I enjoy. It's not always easy of course. Recently, I had to deal with a particularly difficult client who was – fairly unreasonably, it has to be said – very dissatisfied with the solution our sales team had sold them. Rather than let the complaint escalate, I took the time to calmly and patiently listen to the customer and to demonstrate that I understood and empathised with their concerns. This alone took a lot of the wind out of their sails. I went on to give them my viewpoint, addressing their concerns one by one and explaining why I felt the solution they had been sold was the best one for them. It turned out that they had principally misunderstood what was being offered and, once realisation set in, they were actually quite apologetic!

20 How did you get your last job?

Alternative and related questions:

- How did you locate your last job?

The meaning behind the question:
This is a surprisingly popular question among interviewers. The reason is that, whilst seemingly a very simple little question, your answer can give the interviewer insight into numerous different areas. It can help them to assess how much initiative you have, how determined and tenacious you are, how driven you are and how much you plan and control your own career.

Your answer:
You need to realise that there are two different ways of interpreting this question – and you need to make sure that you cover both bases. First of all is the question of how you actually managed to locate your last job (recruitment agency, network contact, speculative application, head-hunted, etc.). Then there is the question of how you went about securing the job – how you convinced the employer that you were the right person for the job. You need to aim to portray an image of somebody in control of their own destiny – not someone who just goes with the flow.

> Example:
> It was actually quite complicated. I was keen for a new challenge and had already started looking around when I saw in the local newspaper that they were opening a new branch in the area. I sent in a speculative application to the HR department at their head office and they wrote back to say that they would only be recruiting through their preferred recruitment agency. So I called them up immediately and, having run through a few key points on my CV, managed to persuade them to at least interview me. They also interviewed a spread of candidates from the recruitment agency but, after a second interview and then a third interview with the Marketing Director herself, I was ultimately offered the job.

21 What does your current job involve on a day-to-day basis?

Alternative and related questions:

- Can you describe an average day in your job?

The meaning behind the question:
They've read your CV; they know what your job involves. Now they want to hear it straight from the horse's mouth. There's nothing more to their question than that – but giving the best answer is a little more complicated.

Your answer:
As I say, the interviewer has read your CV (or application form) so they know more or less what your job entails. It would definitely be a mistake to answer this question by simply reeling off in detail everything you've already stated on your CV. The last thing you want to do is bore the interviewer.

While the description you give on your CV will (and rightly so) be comprehensive, when it comes to answering this question you'd do better to skip a lot of the detail and focus on what's really important – what your job is really about. In particular, you want to focus on areas of your current job which most closely match the job for which you are now applying.

Rather than phrasing your work in terms of duties, try to portray what you do in terms of responsibilities.

> Example:
> My most important responsibility is to achieve sales. I spend most of my day on the shop floor, talking directly to potential customers and trying to establish their needs. I have a very thorough knowledge of our product range so, if they're unsure of their decision, I can give them appropriate advice. I can also steer them towards other – perhaps more expensive – product lines that they haven't already considered. By building rapport with the customer – and addressing any concerns they may have – I have a good chance of closing the sale. I also aim to up-sell on the till where possible, so as to maximise the value of each new customer. Among other responsibilities, I help to control stock levels and liaise with head office accordingly so as to make sure we are neither over-stocked nor under-stocked. I am also involved in the financial management of the branch, working alongside the Branch Manager to put together monthly reports, etc. Given my level of experience, I am also tasked with helping to bring on board new members of staff, training them in our systems and helping them to maximise their sales potential.

22 What contribution do you make to the department in which you work?

Alternative and related questions:

- How does your job relate to the overall goals of your department/organisation?

The meaning behind the question:
The interviewer could have rephrased this question, 'Are you able to see the bigger picture?' They are searching for evidence that you understand the purpose and goals of your department as a whole – and how your role fits into the big scheme of things. While it might not be vital to your ability to undertake your job, it is always preferable for an employee to understand what the overall purpose is of their team or department – and what part they are expected to play in that.

Your answer:
Even if the interviewer hasn't phrased the question so as to use the word 'contribution', you still need to place a clear emphasis in your answer on what it is that you contribute to the overall goals of your department. You've got to demonstrate your value. The interviewer knows what job you perform – but how is it of benefit to your colleagues and to your employer?

Some people won't necessarily work in a specific department as such but, if this is the case for you, then you can simply talk about the contribution you make to other departments and to the organisation as a whole – as in the example below.

Example:
While I am technically part of the IT department, all my colleagues focus very much on keeping the company's computer infrastructure fully functional. However, as the company's only Web developer, I work very much on my own in managing and enhancing the website. I do liaise closely with other departments though, most particularly Marketing and HR. As the website is primarily used as a marketing vehicle and as a way to source new employees, my work is of significant importance to both of these departments. The systems I put in place to collect potential sales leads online make a major contribution to the results of the sales team – these days more and more of our new business comes via the website. And, by identifying ways to attract potential new employees online, I have contributed to a reduction in the amount we spend on recruitment consultants – again resulting in a direct impact on the company's bottom line.

23 What changes have you made to your current job role since you started?

Alternative and related questions:

- How have you changed the job you've been doing?

The meaning behind the question:
All job roles evolve over time – some more than others. The interviewer isn't asking how your job has changed since you were first appointed – they are asking how *you* have changed it. They're looking for evidence of initiative, drive and enthusiasm. The best employees are always looking for ways to make improvements – to change things for the better. It's all too easy for an employee to sit back and just accept things the way they are but that's not the type of employee who is going to help drive an organisation forward.

Your answer:
An interviewer should only be asking this question if your current job is one in which you can reasonably be expected to have made changes to your role.

In many roles there is limited scope for making changes, so your interviewer probably won't be expecting too dramatic an example. If you have been responsible for a tangible improvement to your role then this is obviously going to be an excellent choice. Alternatively, it should be more than sufficient to describe ways in which you took on additional duties and responsibilities that weren't part of your original job description.

Be aware that this is the type of question that an interviewer is particularly likely to check up on when taking up your references – so it's essential to be absolutely honest.

> Example:
> When I first took over the role, I noticed that my predecessor (who was in the job for many years) had been using a number of rather outdated and laborious systems to help him manage the allocation of work to our subcontractors. This was clearly wasting a significant amount of time – and time is money. I therefore consulted with my manager and outlined a proposal to scrap these various manual systems and replace them with a single system running on software I had become adept at using in my previous role. Given the low cost of the software and the obvious advantages of my proposal, my manager agreed to the plan. Having spent a couple of weeks setting up the new system, I consequently reduced my workload substantially and I was able to use this spare time to help my manager with his financial reporting. This gave me useful, additional experience and also freed up my manager to spend more time on other issues.

Word of warning:
For some reason, candidates are particularly prone to misunderstanding this question and interpreting it along the lines of, 'What changes have you made in your current job?' This is a very different question and, no matter how good your answer to this question, your interviewer won't be impressed if you fail to answer the question they actually asked.

24 What did you learn in your last job?

Alternative and related questions:

- What have you learned in each of your previous roles?

The meaning behind the question:
The interviewer could have asked, 'What did you learn in your last job that will be of use to you in this job?' because that is what they are driving at. They are not asking you to talk about your duties, responsibilities or achievements. They are specifically asking in what ways you developed professionally while working in your last job (or any particular job of their choice).

Your answer:
It's vital that your answer should cite one or more examples which are directly relevant to the role for which you are now applying. There's no point in discussing something which isn't going to be of obvious value to you – or, more specifically, your employer – in your next job.

The chances are that your previous role(s) will have prepared you in various ways to meet the challenge of your next job. Try to ascertain what is likely to be most of interest to the interviewer. What are the key requirements of this vacancy? What have you learned that will ensure you meet those requirements? Select at least one – if not two or three – ideas and turn them into strong selling points.

There's no need to highlight how this relates to the role you're applying for. It should be self-evident and, if you make a point of it, there is a risk the interviewer might think you're just saying what they want to hear.

> Example:
> My last job was an excellent learning opportunity and I developed my skills and experience in numerous different ways. While I already had strong IT skills, I didn't have any previous experience of Microsoft Access. When my employer introduced a new order management system which used Access, I was given the opportunity to undertake additional training, so as to be able to work effectively with this. I was then able to put this training into practice on a day-to-day basis and I am now extremely adept at using the package. I also learned a great deal about handling customers. My previous roles were not customer-facing, so it was great to have the chance to develop this area of my experience.

25 Can you tell me about your last appraisal?

Alternative and related questions:

- How was your performance rated in your last appraisal?
- How would you comment on your last appraisal?
- What areas for improvement were identified at your last appraisal?

The meaning behind the question:
Appraisals are supposed to address both your strengths and your weaknesses – both your achievements and your failings. However, the interviewer will know that appraisals focus more on where there is room for improvement than on giving you a pat on the back. This question is a clever ploy to get you to confess precisely where there is room for improvement in your performance.

Your answer:
You're going to need to be careful with your answer to this question. For a start, it's very important to be totally honest – because the interviewer can easily check up on this sort of information when taking up your references and, if it's an internal vacancy for which you are applying, then you can be more or less sure they will already have examined your last appraisal.

It's not a difficult question to get right. You need to focus on the positive points that were brought up in your last appraisal and only touch briefly on any less positive points – making sure that you confirm these are issues you have now addressed or are in the process of addressing. You're under no obligation to relate every last detail of your last appraisal, so I would vote in favour of mentioning several positive points but limiting your answer to cover just one weaker point. If your appraisal brought up an apparent weak point that you can put a positive slant on then so much the better.

Of course, not all employers have a formal appraisal system – and this will certainly simplify your answer! It would, however, be a good idea to mention that, while there was no formal system in place, you have routinely received positive feedback on your performance, both from your boss and from your colleagues.

> Example:
> My last appraisal was very positive. My manager felt that I had made excellent progress in many areas and had really mastered the intricacies of the project we were working on. He did say that he felt other members of the team had become too dependent on me and that a lot of my time was being taken up in showing them how to tackle difficult or unusual issues. While he perceived this as an area for improvement, I perceived this as further evidence that the time is now right for me to take a step up to a management-level position – hence my applying for this role with yourselves.

26 How would you describe your current boss?

Alternative and related questions:

- What do you think of your current boss?
- What kind of relationship do you have with your current boss?

The meaning behind the question:
The interviewer may just be idly curious as to what your current boss is like, but don't count on it. They are much more likely to be probing your perceptions of authority – and, in particular, how you handle authority. While seemingly innocuous, this is actually quite a loaded question. If the interviewer identifies you as having any problems with authority then it's going to be a big black mark on your application.

Your answer:
This is most certainly not the same question as the 'tough' alternative, 'What are your current boss's weaknesses?' that we cover in the next chapter – and you should most certainly be avoiding making any disparaging comments. Regardless of what a loser you might think your boss is, it isn't going to get you anywhere to slate them. Statistically, having problems with their boss is the No. 1 reason people give for changing jobs. However, you'd do well just to give a reasonably complimentary description and portray a positive working relationship between the two of you.

Example:
I'm fortunate to have a pretty positive working relationship with my boss. She gives me a high degree of latitude to get on with my job while always being there to help me with any unusual or difficult situations – to lend me the benefit of her experience. Like many managers, she's often very busy but she does a good job of closely supervising her team, steering us in the right direction and helping us to achieve the results that are expected of us. I know she appreciates the work I do and this obviously helps to motivate me and make me to strive to achieve my very best.

27 Why did you leave that job?

Alternative and related questions:

- Have you ever been made redundant and, if so, why?
- Have you ever been fired?

The meaning behind the question:
This question is distinct from 'Why do you wish to leave your current position?' that we covered in the previous chapter in that it's not exploring your current motivators in changing jobs; it's exploring your previous reasons for having left a job.

The interviewer might also be hoping to turn up any skeletons you may have in your cupboard, for example dismissals.

Your answer:
We've already covered the topic of changing jobs in detail in the previous Chapter under 'Why do you wish to leave your current position?' – and much of that same advice will apply to this question. However, here I'd like to focus on two special cases: two more negative reasons why you might have left a previous job:

- being made redundant
- being fired/sacked.

I would immediately like to apologise to any readers who have been made redundant. It is in no way my intention to cause any offence by listing redundancy as a negative reason for leaving a job. I fully appreciate that redundancy is a difficult time and that there's often little justice in an employer's choice of who to make redundant. I empathise entirely. However, my reason for including it in this list is not to suggest you've been made redundant through any fault of your own – but because your having been made redundant may unfortunately be perceived in a negative fashion by a prospective employer. It is therefore a hurdle you need to deal with – and which I will show you how to deal with.

Redundancy hurts. There's no two ways about it. However, you must conceal any bitterness and resentment you may feel and instead convey to the interviewer that 'such is life', 'these things happen', it wasn't your fault. It is the position that is redundant, not the individual person. Under no circumstances should you criticise the employer that laid you off. Rather than dwell on negative aspects, you must aim to emphasise any positive outcomes – for example that it gave you the opportunity to undertake some valuable training or that it meant you were able to move on to a new and better position.

> Example:
> Unfortunately, a major client, that my department was responsible for supplying, decided to withdraw completely from the UK and close all their branches. It appears they had overreached themselves in deciding to expand beyond the USA. Almost everyone in my department was subsequently made redundant. However, with hindsight, it all worked out very well in the end because I was able to secure a new – and more senior – position within just a couple of months.

If you've been fired from a previous role then this is a tough one to deal with – it's hard to put a positive slant on such matters.

There are two points I need to make about how you should handle this. Firstly, you must be truthful; it's all too easy for a prospective employer to check these sorts of detail. Secondly, you must convey the circumstances as calmly and dispassionately as possible, acknowledge responsibility for the causes of your dismissal and, above all else, convince the interviewer that you learned a great deal from the experience and that this will never, ever happen again.

There are various words and expressions which can be used to describe your being dismissed from a job – sacked, fired, etc. However, these have more negative connotations than simply saying you were dismissed. You should therefore avoid using them in your answer.

Example:
I was only in that job for a couple of months and I unfortunately left it sooner than I would have liked to. I had an initial probationary period of three months and, during that time, I regrettably had an argument with a customer. I felt they were being extremely unreasonable and, rather than pacifying them, I let the situation escalate. It turned out that they were a long-standing customer and they used their influence to insist that my manager dismiss me. I was young and inexperienced and I learnt a great deal from this. I would certainly never now argue with a customer; I know that there are much better ways to resolve such a situation.

BLOOPER!

It's probably a good idea to avoid the following answer given by one candidate: *'The company made me a scapegoat, just like my three previous employers!'*

28 Which of your jobs was the best?

Alternative and related questions:

- What's the best job you have ever had?
- Can you describe the best job you have ever had?
- How would you define your dream job?
- In which job were you the happiest/most fulfilled?

The meaning behind the question:
This is potentially a trick question. Does the interviewer really care which of your jobs was the best? Or are they more interested in identifying what your conception of the perfect job is – and how that matches or differs from the vacancy for which they are currently interviewing you? It's much more likely to be the latter. By identifying what you have most enjoyed in the past they can assess how likely you are to enjoy this job in the future.

Your answer:
You should endeavour to pick a job that is not greatly dissimilar from the one for which you are applying. You then need to explain your choice in such a way as to emphasise the similarities between that role and this current vacancy – subtly of course.

Example:
I have tried to plan my career path carefully, only changing jobs when the right role presented itself. However, I would say my best ever job was my role with Elisabeth Elkins Catering. I was given a considerable degree of autonomy to conceive, plan and implement our marketing strategy. I had a highly productive working relationship with the Managing Director and the outcome was clearly very successful – our sales had more than tripled by the end of my two years.

Word of warning:
Avoid citing your current job. The interviewer will wonder:

- If it's that great then why do you really want to leave?
- If they do give you this job, is there a risk you might later regret it?

29 Why is there a gap in your CV?

Alternative and related questions:

- What did you do during this gap in your employment?
- Can you tell me more about this break in your career history?

The meaning behind the question:
There are two elements here:

- The interviewer will be interested in the reasons for there being a gap in your CV – why you experienced a period of unemployment.
- They will also be interested in what you did during that period of unemployment.

Your answer:
Most people have a gap or two in their career history. It's very common and not normally anything to worry about. There is, however, only one explanation that an employer is really going to view favourably:

- further training/education.

Other common – and conceivably constructive – reasons include:

- raising a child
- caring for another dependant
- travel.

But there are also reasons which will definitely be viewed negatively:

- inability to find a suitable position
- ill health
- imprisonment.

If the reason for the gap in your career history isn't obviously negative then there shouldn't be a gap in your CV – you should have included a brief entry explaining the situation. This will prevent an interviewer from asking you, 'Why is there a gap in your CV?' and will instead prompt them to ask the more positive question, 'Can you tell me more about this break in your career history?'

Further training/education: this is very simple and should already be covered within your CV – but maybe the interviewer has missed it. You need simply politely draw their attention to the further training/education you undertook and use this as an opportunity to talk about why you chose this option and how it adds value to your application.

Raising a child/caring for another dependant: if you took time out of your career in order to care for a family member or close friend then it is very much your own private affair – but one that an interviewer should hopefully view favourably. You should have included a brief entry in your CV explaining the circumstances and the interviewer should refrain from probing too deeply into the matter. The same applies for time out to raise your own family – and I would suggest you refer to the section on sexual discrimination in Chapter 22, 'Illegal questions: and how to dodge them', so that you are fully aware of your rights in this respect.

Travel: taking a sabbatical to go travelling is often seen by an employer as a positive thing. Many will believe that the cultural awareness and sense of independence you will have gained as a result of the experience will prove to be of value to them. Also, if you've already taken time out to travel, then it means you're less likely to suddenly disappear to travel the world just as they've got you settled in. This is a common worry among employers, particularly when it comes to younger employees. If you're questioned on this then it is important to emphasise that it was something you 'needed to do' and now you've 'got it out of your system'. You may also be able to make reference to any temporary and part-time work you undertook in other countries, if that could be an additional selling point for you.

Unfortunately, general unemployment and ill health are unlikely – at least initially – to be viewed favourably by an interviewer. And imprisonment certainly won't be viewed favourably.

Inability to find a suitable position: this is definitely the most common cause for there being a gap in a CV. The problem you face is that if you tell an interviewer you were struggling to find work, then that's inevitably going to worry them. You need to deal with this by explaining carefully that the right job isn't always available at the right time. For further advice on how to handle this please take a look at Question 13, 'You've been out of work for a while. Has it been difficult finding a job?' in the next chapter, Chapter 21, 'The top 25 tough questions: taking the heat'.

Ill health: if you have been absent from work as a result of a significant illness or a major accident then the interviewer should appreciate that these things do happen. For further advice on how to handle questions about your health please take a look at Question 14, 'What's your sickness record like?' in the next chapter.

Imprisonment: this is always going to be an extremely difficult issue to handle and I would suggest you refer to the detailed section on criminal convictions in Chapter 22, 'Illegal questions: and how to dodge them'.

30 What do you know about us as an organisation?

Alternative and related questions:

- What is your impression of our organisation?
- Why do you want to work for this organisation?

The meaning behind the question:
Remember that candidate I mentioned earlier who, famously, upon being asked what he could bring to the company, responded with 'What is it you do again?'

The interviewer wants to make sure you've done your homework, that you really understand what their organisation is all about – and that you consequently have a realistic expectation of what it would be like to work for such an organisation. While they're not going to be deliberately fishing for compliments they will want to ensure that you do have a positive impression of their organisation. Why do you want to work for them in particular?

Your answer:
In the previous chapter we covered the closely related question, 'Why do you want to work for this organisation?' The difference with this question is the greater emphasis you need to place on what you know about the organisation rather than why you want to work for their organisation in particular.

Spell out to the interviewer the key points you know about their organisation – and how you come to know them, for example because you've researched their website, because you've read about them in the newspaper, etc. But don't go into excessive detail.

Make sure that you put a positive spin on any points you raise and, if at all possible, communicate how you feel you are well suited to working for such an organisation.

Avoid saying anything negative or bringing up any bad press, etc. that the organisation may have had.

Example:
I've naturally done some research into your organisation so as to ensure that I fully understand what kind of organisation I would be working for. I read on your website that your sales levels have grown at an average of 25 per cent year on year for the past five years and that you are now working on your expansion into the United States. You're clearly a very progressive organisation and that's exactly what I'm looking for. I want to work for an organisation which doesn't stand still, which is expanding and taking on new and interesting challenges. I've also read a lot of customer comments on various third-party websites and the quality of your service is clearly very impressive.

31 *What do you know about our products/services?*

Alternative and related questions:

- Have you ever bought our products/used our services?

The meaning behind the question:
The interviewer is again testing to see how interested you really are in the vacancy – as defined by the amount of time you have spent researching the operation. Some roles will of course require greater product/service knowledge than others and, if you are applying for a role where such knowledge is critical, for example sales, then the question will take on another dimension. If you can't prove that you fully understand the product/service that the company supplies, then how can you hope to be able to sell it?

Your answer:
If you've prepared properly for your interview then you should be able to demonstrate a reasonably in-depth understanding of the organisation's products/services. The degree to which this will be important will depend on your precise line of work. As well as conveying basic facts it is also a good idea to provide a gentle critique. While you should aim to be more complimentary than critical, if you are able to identify areas for improvement – ideally areas which you yourself would be able to improve – then it is likely to impress the interviewer and count very much in your favour. The best employees rarely accept the status quo; they are always looking for ways to improve things.

Example:
I've actually got one of your posters framed on the wall at home. I was already familiar with the range you offer and, since seeing this vacancy advertised, I have had a closer and more detailed look. I'm naturally impressed by what I've seen. They're printed to a high

degree of quality – something that isn't always the case with posters produced by other companies – and yet they remain very reasonably priced. While you certainly have many interesting – and commercially appealing – designs, I do feel that some parts of the range are becoming a little dated. I would certainly welcome the challenge not only of revamping existing designs within the range but also of further developing the range in new and interesting directions.

32 What do you think are our organisation's greatest strengths, weaknesses, opportunities and threats?

Alternative and related questions:

- What do you think is the greatest advantage we have over the competition?

The meaning behind the question:
This is a complex question. The interviewer wants to really put your knowledge of their organisation – and of the market in general – to the test. Their secondary objective will be to see how you handle a question in four parts: strengths, weaknesses, opportunities and threats. Questions which are really three or four questions in one are often considered to be good basic indicators of intelligence – showing how well your brain can absorb, hold and process multiple concepts simultaneously. Trust me; this is not an easy question – especially when you are already under pressure.

Your answer:
Fear not. Tricky as this question is, if you've prepared for it (which, if you're reading this, you hopefully will have done) then it all boils down to keeping your cool, breaking the question down into its component parts and addressing each of them in turn, one by one. You should also aim to go heavy on the strengths and opportunities, and a little more gently with the weaknesses and threats. It's a big question but try to keep your answer reasonably concise. As with other questions about potentially negative issues, try to put a positive spin on matters. If the role you are being interviewed for could play a part in tackling these weaknesses and threats then make sure you say so.

Example:
I think your greatest strengths are your market-leading position and the customer service philosophy which has resulted in this. Every business has its weakness and I think we'd agree that your greatest weakness is the lack of a comprehensive marketing strategy. As we've already discussed, you focus on a few key marketing avenues

and are leaving a lot of money on the table in certain other areas. I firmly believe this is something I can help you with and that the development of a broad and consistent marketing strategy is consequently also your greatest opportunity. I also feel that expanding internationally represents another major opportunity. As for threats, the greatest threat is quite simply the competition. It's vitally important for you to continue to stay one step ahead of them.

33 *What do you know about the vacancy for which you are applying?*

Alternative and related questions:

- Why have you applied for this vacancy?
- What appeals to you most about this vacancy?

The meaning behind the question:
The interviewer wants to make sure that you really understand the role for which you are applying – and that you fully appreciate what would be involved if you were to be appointed to the role. If you haven't been questioned separately about this, then they will also be trying to glean why it is that you applied for this vacancy and why it appeals to you.

Your answer:
Clearly, if you don't have a reasonably thorough understanding of the role (from the job description or person specification, etc.) then you shouldn't even be at the interview. You need to demonstrate comprehensively to the interviewer that you fully appreciate what the role entails and, ideally, you want to try to pre-empt the next question in this chapter, Question 34, 'How do your skills and experience match the job description/person specification?'

For advice on how to deal with explaining why it is that you have applied for this vacancy – and why it appeals to you – please refer to the separate questions, 'Why have you applied for this vacancy?' in the previous chapter and 'What appeals to you most about this vacancy' – Question 35 below.

Example:
I've carefully studied both the job description and the person specification so I believe I'm fully aware of the precise duties and responsibilities the role entails. You've also helped to clarify a few points during the course of this interview.

You can then go on to deliver your prepared answer to the following question.

34 How do your skills and experience match the job description/person specification?

Alternative and related questions:

- Do you feel your skills and experience match the job description/person specification?
- Do you feel that you have the skills and experience necessary to undertake this job?

The meaning behind the question:
Answering this question is going to be one of your interviewer's primary goals. Many of the other questions will lead them towards an answer but sometimes the interviewer will just come out and ask you directly to tell them how you match the job description/person specification.

As well as helping the interviewer to gauge how well your skills and experience match what they are looking for, this question will normally also reveal a lot about how you perceive the job in question.

Your answer:
You're not going to get away with answering, 'Very well!' to this question. What the interviewer expects you to do – and what you very much need to do – is to explain precisely *how* your skills and experience match the job description/person specification.

Job descriptions and person specifications are often very lengthy and comprehensive. You don't want to go into too much detail when answering this question – not least because it could get rather boring! The best strategy to adopt is for you to select a handful of issues and briefly talk about each in turn – expressing each in terms of your prospective employer's needs.

Naturally, you will need to give this some thought and to have determined in advance what skills and experience the interviewer is going to be most interested in.

> Example:
> I believe my skills and experience are a very good match for the person specification. You're looking for someone with a significant amount of high-level experience in the retail clothing sector. I now have 25 years' experience within this sector, most recently as General Manager of a flagship central London store. You need someone with considerable skill in financial management, able to build turnover – and, most importantly, to build turnover profitably. In my current role my branch now has an annual turnover of £5 million – 40 per cent higher than when I took over the role three years ago. Our profit margin has also grown – from 10 per cent to 15 per cent, meaning that profits have more than doubled in just the last three

years. The role demands an individual who is adept at managing and leading a large team; I'm currently responsible for 65 retail staff. The role also requires an individual who is able to build profitable long-term relationships with key, high-value clients. Successfully catering to the needs of VIP clients is essential to my current role and certainly an aspect that I very much enjoy. Overall, I feel I'm a very good match for the job but would of course be delighted to discuss any particular points in greater detail if you wish.

This answer has obviously been written from the point of view of someone seeking a very senior role. However, the basic principles can easily be adapted to your own precise circumstances. Remember that my examples are purely intended to help illustrate the points made; it's essential for you to think for yourself and to create your own answers.

35 *What appeals to you most about this vacancy?*

Alternative and related questions:

- What are you most looking forward to in this job?
- What is it that you are looking for in a new job?
- Why have you applied for this vacancy?

The meaning behind the question:
This question is similar to the top ten question 'Why have you applied for this vacancy?' that we discussed in the previous chapter. However, it is sufficiently different – and sufficiently popular – to warrant covering it separately.

The interviewer knows that there will be a number of factors which draw you to this vacancy. What they are looking for with this question is to identify your key motivator – what really matters most to you. This will naturally give some insight into you both as a professional and a person.

Your answer:
There's a right way and a wrong way to answer this question. The wrong way is to see matters entirely from your own point of view and to cite some aspect of the vacancy which meets your own needs first and foremost. The right way is to make sure you identify some aspect of the vacancy, which you can talk about in such a way as to place emphasis on how you meet the organisation's needs. The interviewer is more interested in how you meet the company's needs than in how they can meet yours.

Example:
I'm particularly taken with the importance you place on customer service. In too many organisations customer service is very much a secondary priority whereas you place the customer at the centre of

everything you do. As a Customer Service Manager, I am naturally very committed to excellence in customer service – and I am very keen to work with an organisation that attaches the same importance to customer service that I do. A business is nothing without its customers; it's vital to recognise this – and your reputation for customer service is clearly enviable. It sets you apart from the competition.

36 Why have you chosen this line of work?

Alternative and related questions:

- What took you into this line of work?
- What do you like best about this line of work?

The meaning behind the question:
The interviewer could have asked, 'Was it the right choice?' because this is what they are trying to establish – was this the right choice for you and, if so, why? As with almost every other question, the interviewer will be looking for ways in which your answer can be applied to the requirements of the job for which you are applying.

Your answer:
Hopefully you've already gone a long way towards convincing the interviewer that you want this job. Now you need to convince them that this line of work really is the right one for you – in what ways are you best suited to it.

You definitely need to demonstrate enthusiasm for your work – and if you can manage to demonstrate passion then that's even better. Above all you need to show an interest in your line of work and give sound reasons for your having embarked upon this particular career path. Avoid at all costs giving the impression that it is something you just randomly drifted into.

Try to sprinkle your explanation with specific examples of relevant skills and abilities.

Example:
Both my parents are accountants, so I grew up listening to them talking about their work together – and I was always very interested in their working lives. While I considered a range of other options, I've always had a particular talent for mathematics and, ultimately, accountancy was evidently the best choice. I enjoy working with figures; I enjoy applying my mathematical abilities to real-world problems. I also enjoy working with others and find it very rewarding to get to grips with a client's precise circumstances and then help them to find the best solutions to the financial problems they are facing. Accountancy was without doubt the right choice for me.

37 Are there any other organisations to which you are applying?

Alternative and related questions:

- What other organisations are you applying to?
- What other jobs have you applied for?
- Have you had any other interviews yet?
- Have you received any job offers yet?

The meaning behind the question:
This question has nothing directly to do with your ability to do the job. The interviewer is trying to gauge how important this particular application is to you and how much you are in demand with other – possibly competing – organisations. They want to assess how discerning you are or, the other side of the coin, how desperate you are! If you've already received a firm offer from another organisation, then they will know they need to act fast if they don't want to lose you.

Your answer:
You've got to tread carefully here. You don't want to be trapped into disclosing too much detail – especially the names of specific organisations. The only exception to this is if you are also applying to a direct competitor. It's a risky move – the interviewer might see this as rather mercenary on your part – but it can motivate them to want to secure your services rather than let 'the enemy' acquire you. Generally, it's best to dodge the question somewhat and give an appropriately vague answer but, above all, to be truthful. If you round off your answer by emphasising that this particular vacancy is your preferred choice then the interviewer is unlikely to press you for further details of your other applications.

> Example:
> Finding the right position is obviously very important to me, so I am being rather thorough in my job search. I have been quite selective but I have identified a number of different jobs and organisations which fit my criteria, and my applications for these vacancies have reached varying stages. However, this opportunity with yourselves remains my preferred choice – both because of the specifics of the role in question and because the organisation itself is one I feel to be particularly appropriate to me.

38 How does this job compare with others for which you are applying?

Alternative and related questions:

- Why do you want this particular job?
- What most attracts you to this opportunity rather than other vacancies you have applied for?

The meaning behind the question:
This is clearly a more probing question than the previous question and you may well find it being asked as a follow-up to that question. The interviewer is trying to gauge how motivated you are to win this particular role as opposed to one of the others currently open to you. They want to know where they fit on the scale.

Your answer:
You're going to have to tread a fine line here. It's vital to communicate that this job is of course your preferred choice (even if one of the other offers is blatantly superior). However, you most certainly don't want to give the impression that this job is your *only* choice. That would severely weaken your position. The best strategy is to sidestep the question as best you can and focus very much on the vacancy at hand and what most attracts you to this job and to this organisation.

> Example:
> This job clearly has the edge on other applications I am pursuing. I have taken my time to identify a number of possibilities which are closely suited to me – so as not to waste my time or anybody else's. They all have various pros and cons but I am particularly attracted to this job because I feel it offers the best opportunities for me to develop professionally and make a major contribution. It's a perfect match for my skills and experience. I also believe I will fit in very well with the organisation as a whole.

39 Can you describe your ideal employer to me?

Alternative and related questions:

- Which of your employers was the best?

The meaning behind the question:
By identifying what you perceive as the perfect employer, the interviewer can assess how closely their organisation fits this profile – and hence how well you are likely to fit in with the organisation. It's a clever question and

sets a trap that a weaker candidate is likely to walk straight into. If they don't fit your definition of the ideal employer then why would they want to hire you?

Your answer:
It doesn't really matter what your idea of an ideal employer is. What matters is that your description should match the organisation to which you are now applying. Of course, if there's a big difference between your prospective employer and your conception of the ideal employer then you should perhaps be asking yourself whether this is really going to be the right job for you.

The easiest way to tackle this question is to first identify what it is that you like best about your prospective employer – and then build your description of your 'ideal' employer around this.

If you've already prepared an answer to, 'Why do you want to work for this organisation?' (which I covered in the previous chapter) then you can recycle some of the ideas you had for that.

> Example:
> My ideal employer would be a large yet growing company with a strong reputation within its sector, a company which offers plenty of scope for progression within the hierarchy. While my preference is for a larger organisation, I want to work for a company which nevertheless has a dynamic and progressive approach. Your organisation certainly more than meets those requirements.

Word of warning:
It would be inappropriate to openly state that you feel their organisation to be the 'perfect' employer. You will inevitably come across as phoney!

40 What sort of person would you most like to work for?

Alternative and related questions:

- Can you tell me about the best boss you've ever had?
- Putting yourself in your manager's shoes, what is the best way to manage you?

The meaning behind the question:
Along the same lines as the previous question, the interviewer is looking to identify how well you are likely to fit in with your manager. If your prospective manager differs significantly from the description you give, then it's going to raise questions in the interviewer's mind as to how well you are likely to be able to work together.

You should also be aware that the way you answer this question can reveal a lot about what sort of a person you will be to manage.

Your answer:
It's best to avoid going into too much detail and giving too precise a description. Try to keep your answer broad so that it is unlikely to exclude too many people. Horoscopes are carefully written so as to sound meaningful and yet remain as vague as possible – so that they can be seen to be pertinent by as many people as possible. You want to adopt the same tactic.

By phrasing your answer carefully, you can also score a few discreet points with regard to what sort of a person you are like to work with. Try to convey the impression that you'd most like to work for someone who was a lot like you – and then give a positive description of that person.

> Example:
> I'd most like to work for someone who has the same approach as I do to getting things done – planning, organisation and action. Also, I'm always keen to take on new duties and responsibilities so I'd welcome a manager who was prepared to give me the chance to continue my professional development. Besides this, a good manager is of course always approachable, supportive and sensitive to the needs of their team; while I'm good at working on my own initiative, every team needs a leader to give it direction.

41 In what ways is your degree relevant to the work you are now doing?

Alternative and related questions:

- Why did you choose to study *x* at university and how do you feel it is relevant to this job?
- What did you learn at university that will help you to undertake this job?

The meaning behind the question:
Completing a degree course is a significant undertaking. In asking this question the interviewer is trying to appreciate what your degree course involved and how the skills and experience gained during your time at university will be of use in the job for which you are now applying.

Your answer:
The way you answer this question will depend on your circumstances – and there are two main possibilities.

If your degree is directly relevant to the work you are now doing – for example if you're a doctor – then this question is reasonably straightforward to answer. You just need to pick a few key aspects of your degree course which you have found to be particularly useful to you in your working life. Describe these briefly and demonstrate the bearing they have on your suitability for the role for which you are applying.

If, however, your degree was in Criminology and you are now working as a Finance Assistant, then talking about the module on 'Criminal Justice in Modern Britain' is obviously going to be completely irrelevant! Instead, in such cases, you should be concentrating on:

- What transferable skills and abilities you developed during your degree course.
- How these skills and abilities relate to your current line of work.
- How the experience of completing a degree course has helped you develop as an individual.

Many employers are sceptical as to the real-world value of some degree courses. There is a common perception that graduates lack initiative – and the ability to apply their theoretical knowledge to practical purposes. Make sure you dispel any doubts the interviewer may have in this respect.

> Example:
> While my degree in Geography is of course not directly relevant to my current role as a Market Researcher, it was nevertheless a very worthwhile experience in many different ways. I developed a broad set of transferable skills, including how to compile, interpret and analyse data – skills I now apply on a daily basis. I also undertook a number of team projects, working together to achieve a goal, including writing up the results of our findings – and how best to structure and communicate our arguments. Undertaking a degree course was, of course, a major personal challenge and I definitely matured significantly during my time at university – learning how to plan and organise my own workload so as to meet all my deadlines. I feel it has definitely helped to prepare me for my current career.

42 What have you learned and how have you developed over the last year/five years?

Alternative and related questions:

- What did you learn in your last job?
- What did you learn in each of your previous roles?

The meaning behind the question:
Ongoing personal and professional development is vital in many different lines of work. The interviewer will be looking for:

- Evidence that you are someone who takes their continuing development seriously.
- Details of how you have developed in ways which will be useful in your next job.

Your answer:
This question is similar to Question 24, 'What did you learn in your last job?' but is sufficiently different for us to handle it separately. Yes, the interviewer will be interested in what you have learned in your last job, but this is a broader question and requires a broader answer – particularly if the interviewer has asked about the past five years instead of just the last 12 months.

You may have developed in numerous ways during the past five years but you should endeavour to select examples which are directly relevant to the role for which you are now applying. Talk about general ways in which you've developed as an individual, talk about specific training you have undertaken – and above all make it clear that you have been the driving force behind your development, not your employers.

> Example:
> Over the course of the past five years, I have made an effort to develop my skills and experience in numerous different ways. I have matured as an individual and my experience of working with others – both colleagues and customers – has contributed a lot to my interpersonal skills. I am also better able to see the bigger picture and how my role relates to the overall goals of the organisation. Having built up a broad range of experience, I am now much more productive in my role – and much better equipped to handle unusual or difficult situations. In terms of training, I have learned a range of new IT skills, including Microsoft PowerPoint and Microsoft Access. I have also undertaken an evening course in business administration, which has helped to shape the way I work and has given a formal structure to many of the skills I was already developing on a practical basis. I am also now a qualified First Aider.

43 What sports are you/have you been involved in?

Alternative and related questions:

- Do you play any sports?

The meaning behind the question:
It's hard to say what the interviewer's precise motivations are in asking you this question. There are a number of possibilities; it depends on the interviewer. All interviewers will be looking for evidence that you are a fit and physically active individual. Some will also be looking to gauge whether or not you are a 'team player' – or even a team leader. And others will be trying to identify a competitive streak. However, there's actually no evidence that individuals who play sports are any more competitive or any more likely to work well in a team than those who never go near a pair of trainers!

Your answer:
If you are involved in any sports then it should already say so on your CV – and the interviewer should therefore know this. In asking you this question, they're consequently expecting you to elaborate on what you've stated on your CV.

If you're fortunate enough to be captain of the local football team then, besides the obvious selling point of football being a team activity (and your hence being a 'team player'), you've immediately got an opportunity to communicate your leadership qualities, your ability to take responsibility for others, your ability to commit yourself to a project, etc.

However, if, like many of us, you rarely find time to engage in any sporting activity, then there's no need to fear. This question is unlikely to be a deciding factor in whether or not you get the job. Stick to the truth and try to mention at least one physical activity, even if it's just walking in the park at the weekend!

> Example:
> There's currently little routine to my life. Business needs are such that I travel very frequently and consequently work irregular hours. This leaves little room for me to participate in any sporting activities. However, I do like to keep myself fit and healthy and, if at all possible, I take the opportunity to go for a walk in the morning before I start work. This helps to wake me up, get some oxygen into my brain and I also use the time to think through the day ahead of me and what it is that I need to achieve. I'm aware that there's a lot less travel involved in this job, so this means I may have more opportunity in the future to play tennis again.

44 Do you know what the current headline news is?

Alternative and related questions:

- What news story has interested you recently?

The meaning behind the question:
Apart from a handful of professions, for example journalism, this question is likely to have precious little to do with your ability to perform the job – unless it's your particular industry or line of work that's been in the news. Instead, the question is more about the interviewer trying to understand what sort of person you are – how much active interest you take in the world around you and the society you live in. This gives the interviewer greater insight into your character and helps them to assess how well you will fit in with your prospective future colleagues and with their organisational culture. The interviewer might also want to get your opinion on the matter – so as to test your analytical skills.

Your answer:
'No' is not an option. Whether or not you're interested in current affairs you need to make sure you're reasonably clued up on what's going on in the world whenever you're attending interviews. It's a simple enough matter to buy a daily newspaper (avoiding the tabloids) or to watch the news on television. Avoid being controversial; avoid saying too much – but do volunteer a brief opinion on the matter if it's appropriate to do so. As well as this being a 'formal' question that might come up at interview, the interviewer could easily make reference to some newsworthy topic in the 'small talk' phase before – or, indeed, after – an interview. If you haven't got the faintest idea what they're talking about then it's not going to make a good impression.

> Example:
> I like to keep abreast of current affairs – mainly via the BBC News website, which gives me a thorough but balanced overview. The major news at the moment remains the ongoing conflict in the Middle East. It's a tragic situation and it's very hard to see what the long-term solution is going to be, so deep-rooted are the problems.

45 How quickly can you adapt to a new work environment?

Alternative and related questions:

- How long does it generally take you to settle into a new work environment?
- How long do you feel it will take you to make an impact in your new job?

The meaning behind the question:
Whenever someone takes up a new role, it will inevitably take them some time to settle in. If you've been in your previous job for a number of years,

then it can be quite a shock to the system starting a new job – and you'd be surprised how many employees walk out within their first week! The interviewer isn't necessarily asking you for a precise timescale as to how long you'll take to settle in. What they really want from you is evidence that you understand the upheaval involved in changing jobs and that you are prepared for this and will consequently adapt to your new situation as quickly as possible.

Your answer:
Above all, you must convey to the interviewer that you are able to adapt quickly to new circumstances. However, more than that, you should attempt to convey why you will be able to adapt quickly to new circumstances. It's all very well to say that you will adapt quickly but it doesn't mean very much unless you can back up your statement with some convincing evidence.

The best way to handle this is to refer to your current or previous job and how quickly you were able to settle in there.

If this is your first job then you could instead refer to how you handled the start of your degree course – or how you settled into your last school.

> Example:
> I believe I've very good at adapting to changes in my circumstances. While every organisation is different and no two jobs I've had have ever been the same, the core requirements of my role don't change. I appreciate that there will inevitably be new procedures that I need to absorb and adhere to – and it also takes time to forge positive working relationships with new colleagues. However, I don't anticipate it taking very long at all before I'm fully up to speed and making a major contribution. When I took up my current role, I'd been with my previous employers for more than five years. It was clearly a major change for me. I nevertheless settled in very quickly, got to know my colleagues and to understand the way the organisation worked – and I already felt quite at home before the end of my first month.

46 Would it be a problem if we asked you to work overtime/evenings/weekends?

Alternative and related questions:

- Would it be a problem for you to take work home occasionally at the weekend?
- Do you have a preference for working regular days and hours?
- How do you feel about the amount of overtime this role demands?

The meaning behind the question:
In some jobs it is going to be essential for you to work unusual hours – and if that's the case the interviewer probably wouldn't even be asking you the question. In other lines of work there will be an unspoken expectation that you will be prepared to put in longer hours than the average. Generally, an interviewer is most likely to be asking you this question if working overtime/evenings/weekends isn't in fact the norm for your job. They want to identify how flexible you are in terms of accommodating the company's needs even when it might be to your own detriment – in other words how committed you are to your work.

Your answer:
It is of course entirely up to you how you feel about working above and beyond 'normal' office hours. There will be numerous factors you have to weigh up and the decision is yours alone.

Once you have established your position on the matter, honesty is very much the best policy. Unfortunately, it may well count against you if you're unwilling – or quite simply unable – to work long hours. But don't let yourself be talked into accepting working conditions which you know you won't be happy with unless you really are prepared to live up to your promises.

Whatever your stance, try to communicate your opinion in as reasonable and positive a manner as possible. Even if you aren't keen on overtime, you might be prepared to offer a compromise as in the example below.

> Example:
> I'm reasonably flexible and if business needs are such that it would be advantageous for me to worker longer hours – and even weekends – then, depending on my other commitments, I would certainly be prepared to do so. However, I would hope that this would be the exception rather than the rule. I do believe in a life outside of work and, whilst my job is clearly very important to me, I would generally like to keep my working hours within normal bounds. In my current role I have had to put in some overtime during especially busy periods – and I have had no objections to doing so. However, I am efficient and productive and I generally manage to complete my work without having to resort to overtime.

47 What is your current salary package?

Alternative and related questions:

- How much are you currently earning?

The meaning behind the question:
Very simple. The interviewer wants to establish what level of remuneration you currently enjoy and see how that compares to the package their organisation is planning to offer (which may or not have been previously disclosed).

Your answer:
Your answer is also very simple. I would strongly recommend against any answer other than the absolute truth. They're not asking what salary package you are now looking for (that's the next question in this chapter). They're asking what you currently receive and that's what you need to tell them, although it's always a good idea to emphasise that money is not your only motivator. When it comes to talking money, you never want to come across as mercenary. (The only exception to this would be for those working in sales and other money-driven and largely commission-based roles.)

> Example:
> I currently have a basic salary of £32,200 with a Ford Mondeo company car. I also receive an annual bonus; this year it was £2,500. While my remuneration is clearly important, it's most certainly not the only deciding factor in my choice of a new job and a new employer. Continuing my professional development within a suitably challenging role is also very important to me.

48 What salary package are you expecting for this role?

Alternative and related questions:

- What would you consider to be an appropriate rate of remuneration for this job?

The meaning behind the question:
There's nothing complicated about this. Regardless of what you're currently earning the interviewer wants to identify what it is that you want in order to work for their organisation – and to assess how that fits in with what they're prepared to offer.

Your answer:
This is not nearly so simple to answer as the previous question. You need to have thought through very carefully in your own mind both what salary package you can reasonably expect and also what the minimum is that you would be prepared to accept, assuming the job itself was suitably attractive. These are issues only you can decide but it will certainly help to have an awareness of what your 'market value' really is. This will take a little research. But that's not to say you should give a precise answer. Unless you have a firm job offer in hand, it's best to dodge the question slightly and quote a range of possibilities.

Example:
The opportunities I'm currently pursuing generally involve salary packages between £35K and £40K and I am comfortable with this range. While the salary on offer won't necessarily be the deciding factor in my choice, I am naturally keen to achieve a position which offers nearer the high end of this scale – a package which best reflects my worth.

49 When would you be available to start?

Alternative and related questions:

- What notice period does your current contract stipulate?

The meaning behind the question:
Sorry, this doesn't necessarily indicate that you've won the job! The interviewer is generally just planning ahead and trying to identify when, if you were to be offered the job, you would be able to start work. It's a simple, factual question.

Your answer:
Your answer is going to be relatively straightforward. Stick to the facts. Tell the interviewer what your current notice period is and how many leave days you remain entitled to – since these could reduce your notice period. You should also have decided in advance whether you wish to take advantage of the break between jobs to have a week or two's holiday.

Bear in mind that if the interviewer urgently needs to fill the vacancy then the time frame within which you are able to start may be a deciding factor.

However, most employers are generally very understanding of notice periods and will be prepared to wait if it means they secure the best candidate for the job.

In some circumstances you may even wish to give your current employer more time to replace you than is stipulated in your contract. While this might be inconvenient for your next employer, they may well be impressed by your loyalty and dedication. This should be negotiable anyway and, if it does pose a major problem for your prospective employers, they will simply tell you.

Example:
My current contract stipulates a notice period of four weeks but I fortunately have ten days' leave available to me, which effectively reduces my notice period to just two weeks. On receipt of a firm job offer I would intend to resign immediately from my current position and conceivably start my new role just two weeks later.

50 Do you mind if we contact your current employer for a reference?

Alternative and related questions:

- Would you give us permission to take up appropriate personal and professional references?

The meaning behind the question:
While the interviewer's interest in checking your references is certainly not a negative sign, it's still not yet a job offer. Most employers (if they have any sense) will take up references before hiring someone. It's always a sensible precaution.

Your answer:
You don't want your referees to be pestered unnecessarily by time wasters. By the time they have handled their umpteenth enquiry of the day, they are a lot less likely to say nice things about you! This is consequently not as straightforward a question to answer as it might at first seem. Your answer needs to be phrased in such a way as to make it clear that you have nothing to hide and you would be quite happy to provide details of referees but that this should only be done once your application is subject to a firm job offer. This is an entirely reasonable request and deserves to be respected.

> Example:
> I understand the importance of references and would be delighted for you to have a word with my referees – I'm confident they'll be very supportive of my application. However, because my decision to change jobs is quite a sensitive issue – particularly with regard to my current employer – I would of course prefer if we could leave the issue of referees until such time as we might be discussing a firm job offer.

Chapter **21**

The top 25 tough questions: taking the heat

I made the point in the previous chapter that many questions which you might initially believe to be 'tough' are actually just more aggressively phrased versions of classic questions. Any questions which neatly fit this definition we have covered in detail in the last chapter.

Unfortunately, the fact remains that there are a number of questions which can only be defined as tough, mean or downright nasty!

There's absolutely no need to panic though. As always, preparation is the key. If you're aware that you might get asked a particular question and you've taken the time to think it through beforehand and prepare an answer then you've won more than half the battle.

One of the main reasons interviewers ask such questions is to throw candidates off balance. I remember, early in my career, one interviewer asking me bluntly, 'Can you make tea?'! They also want to see how they react under stress and pressure. It is of course essential that you remain calm under fire and don't give the interviewer the impression that you've been rattled in any way. If you're prepared for the question then you'll obviously be a whole lot less likely to panic.

Turning negatives into positives

An identifying feature of tough interview questions is that they will either address a negative issue or will be phrased in such a manner as to lead you into giving what seems to be a negative response.

The key to all answers is to identify how you can turn this potentially negative situation into a positive one – which really isn't too difficult when you know how.

No beating about the bush

Another identifying feature of many tough interview questions is how direct they are. They're often very lacking in subtlety. They come straight to the point and put you instantly on the spot. Rather than seeing this as a threat you should try to see it as something positive; at least you're unlikely to misunderstand the question!

1 You must surely have more than one weakness?

The meaning behind the question:

I mentioned in an earlier chapter that you should be prepared for the interviewer to ask the follow-up question, 'OK. That's one weakness. You must surely have more than one weakness?'

What they're doing with this question is trying to put you under pressure to see how you react. Most people attending an interview will have prepared one stock answer to the question, 'What are your weaknesses?' – which will cover talking about just one weakness. They're not expecting to have to:

- think of a second weakness
- let alone talk about it!

Your answer:
Like many so-called 'tough' questions, this is only really a tough question if you haven't prepared for it. Your answer is easy enough and should be prepared along the same lines as you will already have prepared for the top ten question, 'What are your weaknesses?' that we discussed in Chapter 19, 'The top ten interview questions'. However, you have a lot more leeway to cite an example that really isn't a weakness at all.

> Example:
> I suppose everybody has more than one weakness. If I had to think of another weakness I would say it's that I have a tendency to focus too much on detail. I can go to great lengths to get something just right – and this can of course mean that it takes me somewhat longer to complete than someone who rushes the task. However, I very much believe that if something is worth doing then it is worth doing to the very best of your ability. Also, it's well known that cutting corners can just lead to more work in the long term; it's counterproductive.

Word of warning:
If you're up against a particularly difficult interviewer then it's always possible they will press you to give yet another example. As always, the secret is to be prepared.

2 *What character flaws do you have?*

Alternative and related questions:

- Do you have any personality defects?

The meaning behind the question:
This is an aggressively phrased – and potentially very leading – question. The interviewer is trying to force you to expose a major weakness. It's not too dissimilar to their questioning you about your weaknesses except that

it's a much broader question – and a much more personal question. While they will obviously be interested in any personality defects you may have, the main purpose in asking you this question is to put you in a difficult situation and see how you handle it.

Your answer:
It would most likely be a fatal error to respond directly to this question and start talking about something which is inherently going to be very negative. While declaring that you have no weaknesses would be excessive, it is perfectly reasonable to state that you don't feel you have any character flaws. You can instead sidestep the question so as to talk about a more minor weakness and, as always when discussing potentially negative points, make sure you put some spin on it so as to turn a negative into a positive.

> Example:
> Everybody's character is different of course but I don't believe I have any major character flaws. I suppose I can, on occasion, be overly demanding – both of myself and members of my team. I can be very critical of my own work and I expect those under me to work to the same standards. I am nevertheless a patient individual and am prepared to give members of my staff a reasonable chance. Everyone makes mistakes – the important thing is never to make the same mistake twice.

3 *How do you handle being criticised?*

Alternative and related questions:

- How do you take criticism?
- How did you react when you were last criticised?
- Can you tell me about an occasion when your work was criticised?
- Have you ever had an idea that has been criticised by someone else?

The meaning behind the question:
Hearing you describe how you handle criticism will tell the interviewer a lot about you as a person – and about what sort of person you are to work with. Everybody needs to be prepared to accept criticism – constructive criticism – where it is due. The interviewer won't want to hire someone who reacts badly to criticism – someone who isn't prepared to listen to criticism or someone who takes it as a personal attack. If you have a problem with criticism then you're going to be difficult to manage – and you're not going to get the job.

Your answer:
While it can be a good idea (even if you haven't specifically been asked to do so) to cite an example of a situation where you were criticised, you will need to choose your example very carefully – don't pick a major blunder – and make sure you phrase it in such a way as to demonstrate that you learned from the experience.

Yet again, you need to take what could potentially be a negative topic and turn it around so that it becomes a positive selling point. Don't fall into the trap of exposing a weakness. As always, make sure you come up smelling of roses!

For those of you who do have a problem with criticism, it doesn't really matter how you handle criticism – it's how you lead the interviewer to believe that you handle criticism which really counts!

> Example:
> If criticism is due then I generally welcome it. I'm very critical of my own work and I always appreciate constructive criticism and feedback from others, especially those who may have a different angle on matters or possibly more experience than I do. I was recently asked to work on a tender document for a new contract and, since this is not normally a part of my job, my experience in this respect is naturally limited. I consequently actually invited criticism from both my line manager and from a more experienced colleague. While they were largely impressed with my work they certainly gave me constructive criticism on a number of different areas and this helped me to perfect the document. We won the contract and I've definitely learned a lot from the experience, which will be useful to me in the future.

4 *What really makes you lose your rag?*

Alternative and related questions:

- What causes you to lose your temper?
- What really makes you angry?
- Do you ever lose your cool?

The meaning behind the question:
The gloves are off. This is a very direct and potentially very challenging question. The interviewer will know that they are immediately putting you under pressure with such a question. And that's very appropriate – because this question is all about pressure, what causes you to feel under pressure and how you react under excessive levels of stress and pressure. Your answer could tell the interviewer a lot about yourself.

Your answer:
This is one question where it would definitely be best not to give a specific example! The interviewer will not be impressed by hearing about the time you stubbed your cigarette out in your manager's coffee cup before telling him precisely where he could stick his job! Regardless of how volatile your character is, you need to convey an impression of a calm, level-headed individual – and one who remains as such even when the going gets tough. Everybody loses their rag sometimes – including the interviewer sitting opposite you – but it would be a fatal mistake for you to disclose too much about yourself with your answer.

> Example:
> I recognise that losing my temper is very unlikely to achieve anything – in fact getting angry is generally very counterproductive. While the behaviour of others can of course sometimes cause me to feel frustrated or even annoyed, I always focus on remaining calm and finding solutions to the problem at hand. I try to channel any negative feelings into my work because that's normally the best way of resolving the issue. Stress and pressure are a fact of life, and losing your rag won't fix anything.

5 How did you cope with the most difficult colleague you've ever had?

Alternative and related questions:

- Have you ever had problems getting on with a colleague?
- Is there anyone you currently work with that you find really difficult to relate to?
- What sort of person do you find it difficult to work with?
- Have you ever had to work with someone really difficult?

The meaning behind the question:
The way in which you answer this question will tell the interviewer pretty much everything they need to know about your interpersonal skills.

When it comes to dealing with interpersonal conflict, there are three main ways in which you might react:

- Do you clash head-on with difficult people?
- Do you find ways of dealing with them?
- Do you run away and hide?

The interviewer wants to ascertain which of these categories you fall into. It's a probing question that will not only tell them how you are likely to interrelate with your colleagues but will also speak volumes about your character in general.

Whilst it might seem blatantly obvious what makes someone difficult to work with, the interviewer will also be interested in your perception of what makes a colleague difficult.

Your answer:
The correct answer is, of course, to convey to the interviewer that you fall firmly into the second category. You want to demonstrate that you are someone who, when faced with a difficult colleague (or customer, for that matter) will find ways to deal with them – and to put your relationship on a more positive footing. It's a great opportunity to portray yourself as management material.

The interviewer won't want to hire a hothead who is just going to clash with their colleagues, nor do they want to hire someone who is going to be prone to being bullied. Most working environments contain at least one 'difficult' person – it's the school bully syndrome. It's a fact of life and you've got to show that you can cope with it – not only that you can cope with it but that you can, in spite of the difficulties, work successfully with such individuals.

Empathy is very important but it's vital to be assertive with it or you're not going to get very far.

Example:
Like everybody, I've certainly had to deal with difficult colleagues on occasion – colleagues who have failed to pull their weight, who have been too ready to blame others for their errors or who simply have an unpleasant and unprofessional attitude. I'm not afraid of making my opinion known and I believe that communication – especially in difficult or high-pressure situations – is essential in developing effective working relationships. While some interpersonal conflict is inevitable, I don't believe in clashing head-on with difficult colleagues. It's much more productive to try to understand them, to reason with them and to find ways of working through any difficulties you may have. Communication is the key. You often find that someone with whom you initially had difficulties can, once you've reached an understanding, become a valued co-worker.

6 Are you able to make difficult decisions and tough choices?

Alternative and related questions:

- Have you ever had to make a really difficult decision at work?
- What kind of decisions do you find difficult?
- Have you ever had to make a tough and unpopular choice at work?

The meaning behind the question:
You might think that there's no hidden meaning to this question – that it's a very direct question as to your decision-making abilities. However, it all hinges on precisely how you define a difficult decision – and your answer will almost inevitably reveal this. The interviewer wants to assess what your conception of a difficult decision is – and how you feel about making such decisions.

Your answer:
The secret is to establish your definition of a difficult decision. Some decisions are inevitably more difficult to make than others – but you don't want to lead the interviewer into believing you would have problems making a difficult decision if it was necessary. Rather than betraying indecisiveness (which will always be a negative point) you need to demonstrate you accept that it is a necessary evil to have to make certain difficult decisions.

This question is most likely to be asked of those in reasonably senior positions – as the saying goes, it's tough at the top. It's therefore a good idea to focus on decisions which have a direct impact on the lives of your staff – undoubtedly the most difficult decisions any manager has to make. Most managers will, at one stage or another, have had to fire someone or make someone redundant – or at the very least take the decision to discipline a member of staff.

> Example:
> For me, the most difficult decisions are those with the highest human cost, for example the decision to make redundancies. However, I don't shy away from my responsibilities and I recognise that certain business circumstances can force such decisions – and that it would be potentially fatal not to make such decisions firmly and efficiently. In the last recession I had to make a number of redundancies as a result of the adverse economic climate. I certainly wouldn't claim it was easy – but it was necessary to protect the business and the livelihoods of everyone else working for the organisation.

7 *Why haven't you achieved more in your career?*

Alternative and related questions:

- Why haven't you achieved more in your current/last job?

The meaning behind the question:
This question is clearly a veiled criticism. It's a very clever question and can quickly separate out the weaker candidates from the stronger ones. This is a tough question because the main aim of the question is to put you under pressure – under attack – so as to see how you handle it. As with a number of other tough questions, the way you answer is more of interest to the interviewer than an actual explanation as to why you haven't achieved more.

Your answer:
Don't let this question rattle you. Don't let the interviewer put you on the defensive. Don't take it personally.

In most cases, you shouldn't fall into the trap of admitting that you feel you should have achieved more. Even Bill Gates will feel he should have achieved more in his career; it's human nature to feel you could have done better. You should instead spin this question around and throw it back at the interviewer as a statement of precisely what it is you have achieved in your career – and why you are proud of that. You should also express optimism for the future.

If, on the other hand, you clearly could have achieved more in your career, then you should attempt to cite some extenuating circumstances. This is inevitably going to be a weaker answer but it's preferable to stubbornly insisting that there aren't any weaknesses in your career path when there blatantly are. It's even more important in this case to express your optimism for the future – to emphasise that you are now 'back on track' and ready to make up for lost time.

> Example:
> I'm actually very pleased with my career to date. As I've progressed from organisation to organisation I've gained a great deal of practical experience and developed my abilities considerably. I have been responsible for a number of significant achievements; in my current role I successfully drove down stock from £1.5 million to £800K in just nine months – while maintaining lead times – consequently boosting working capital by £700K. I always strive to achieve my best and that is definitely a factor in my now looking for a new job. I feel that this vacancy would be a perfect next step for me because I know I can rise to the challenge and make a major contribution.

8 *What don't you like about this line of work?*

Alternative and related questions:

- What aspects of your job would you change if you could?

The meaning behind the question:
This is a loaded question designed to talk you into disclosing potentially negative information about your attitude to your work. The interviewer is trying to gain further insight into how suited you are to this line of work – and in particular how suited you are to the vacancy for which you are now applying.

Your answer:
This can be a slippery question to answer but it's not really that difficult to get right if you understand the meaning behind the question and are able to avoid various pitfalls.

First of all, you're not going to get away with replying, 'Nothing at all.' Everybody has some aspects of their work that they don't like – or at least like less than other parts. Even film stars must get fed up with having to be on set at 5 am in order to earn their £10 million fee!

Having established that you've got to come up with at least one aspect of your work that you're not mad about, it is essential to make sure you pick on something minor. After all, if there's something major you don't like about this line of work then why are you applying for this job? Preferably you should hit on one or two minor issues which almost everyone in your line of work is likely to also find objectionable.

The main thrust of your answer has to be that you do of course very much enjoy this line of work and that any downsides are only minor. As usual, turn an inherently negative question around so as to give a positive reply. Downplay your dislikes so that they appear trivial and irrelevant.

> Example:
> I love this line of work and so it's hard for me to say there are areas of it that I don't like – but there are naturally some areas I enjoy less than others. They're very minor though. For example, while I appreciate the importance of adhering to the requirements of all the compliance legislation it does take up time that I would rather spend actually working with clients to find solutions to their problems. It can also be frustrating dealing with call-centre staff at the banks because they rarely seem to have the knowledge or authority to resolve a situation and this is a further waste of time that could otherwise be better spent.

9 Where does your current employer think you are at the moment?

Alternative and related questions:

- What reason did you give to your current employer for your being absent to attend this interview?
- Why does your current boss think you're not at work right now?

The meaning behind the question:
Ouch! This really can be a nasty question. As well as being a deliberate attempt to panic you, the interviewer is also probing both your loyalty and your honesty. They'll be very interested to find out both how you handle the question and where, indeed, your current employer does think you are.

Your answer:
If you're lucky, your boss will know exactly where you are and your answer will be a piece of cake. In most cases, though, your boss will be blissfully unaware of what you are up to – and you could have given any one of a number of excuses as to where you are. The single most important thing here is to not be exposed as a liar. You may have made up a little white lie for your current employer to explain your absence – it's harmless enough. But it's not going to impress your interviewer. I hate to say it but it'll be time to cover one little white lie with another.

> Example:
> For obvious reasons, I haven't told my current employer about this interview. I consider it, for the time being, to be a personal matter and that's precisely what I told my boss – that I would be needing to take a half-day today because I had a personal matter to attend to.

10 What are your current boss's weaknesses?

Alternative and related questions:

- What's the main criticism you would make of your current boss?

The meaning behind the question:
This is a very thorny question – and the interviewer knows it to be a very thorny question. It's unlikely they care very much about what your boss's weaknesses are – although they will be interested in seeing how you define weakness. But, as with many of the toughest questions, the interviewer is primarily interested in how you react to the question.

Your answer:
It would be a mistake to say that your boss has no weaknesses; it'll ring hollow. However, it would also be a mistake to level too much criticism at your boss – because you won't come across as being a very loyal employee, because it has no relevance to your ability to do the job for which you are applying and because it's quite simply unprofessional. You want to deflect this question and the secret is to tackle the question along much the same lines as you would respond to the question, 'What are your weaknesses?' Talk about a weakness that's not necessarily a weakness at all – but make it sound convincing!

> Example:
> I'd naturally be wary of criticising my boss because I don't think it's very professional. However, everyone has their weaknesses of course. My boss wouldn't be in the role she's in if her strengths didn't significantly outweigh her weaknesses. If I had to cite a weakness I would say it's that she tends to bite off more than she can chew. I don't know if it's necessarily a weakness to be overly ambitious but, as a result, she does often seem excessively busy and overworked and, inevitably, certain items slip through the net. However, the net result is probably she they gets a lot more accomplished than the average person.

11 What are your current employer's plans for the year ahead?

Alternative and related questions:

- Is your current employer planning to launch any new products/services?
- Is your current employer planning to expand this year?

The meaning behind the question:
There are two possible scenarios here. The interviewer could simply be attempting to assess how professional you are in terms of loyalty, discretion, honesty, etc. Alternatively, they could be deliberately pumping you for commercially sensitive information. Sadly it is the case that some interviews are purely a pretext for extracting information from a competitor's employees. It may be hard to tell which of the two scenarios you are in but it doesn't really matter because the answer you need to give is the same.

Your answer:
It's very simple. You should in no way be divulging your current employer's confidential plans. If there are any plans for new products, services, etc.

which are already clearly in the public domain then you can of course talk about that. But you should resist all temptation to let the interviewer extract any other information from you. While they might lead you to think it will be to your advantage to spill the beans, at the end of the day nobody wants to employ someone who could later pose a security risk.

Example:
I regret that any of my current employer's plans are of course confidential and commercially sensitive. I'm naturally honour bound not to divulge details. I'm sorry. I would of course be more than happy to talk about how the business has developed over the past 12 months and the role I played in that.

12 *What reservations do you have about working for us?*

Alternative and related questions:

- Can you see any disadvantages to working for us?
- Have you ever heard anything negative about our organisation?

The meaning behind the question:
The interviewer is laying a trap for you here. By assessing what reservations you might have about the organisation, they can gauge how much the position really appeals to you. If the interviewer can identify you as having any concerns or reservations about working for the organisation then they're immediately going to have concerns as to your commitment to wanting to work for the company.

Your answer:
There's only one way to answer this question: You don't have any reservations. And then go on to explain why you don't have any reservations – or, more specifically, to reiterate what it is that attracts you to this organisation.

If you do have any reservations – or have heard bad things about the organisation – then you should certainly keep these to yourself, but you should also be asking yourself why you would want to be working for this organisation if you have such concerns.

I know some readers will feel that it is only natural to have some doubts about a potential employer and that it is therefore reasonable to bring these up at interview, albeit in a polite and positive manner. I can see where you're coming from on this – but if you do take this path then be warned that you are treading on very thin ice. I would vote very much in favour of sidestepping this question.

Example:
I don't have any reservations. I've done my research and considered the matter in detail and I have concluded that this is an excellent opportunity – and one which I am eager to pursue. Yours is a rapidly growing and dynamic organisation and I am sure I will fit in well here.

13 *You've been out of work for a while. Has it been difficult finding a job?*

Alternative and related questions:

- Why have you been out of work for so long?
- Why were you out of work for so long between these two jobs?

The meaning behind the question:
If it's been a while since you last worked then there could be many different reasons. The interviewer wants to know precisely what the reason is and what, if any, bearing it has on your application.

Your answer:
The most common reason for being out of work is, surprise, surprise, because you have been struggling to find work. But if you tell the interviewer this then it will immediately ring alarm bells. It may seem harsh, but if nobody else wants you then why should they?

You need to chose your words carefully so as to convey the impression that the reason you have been out of work is not because your services are not in demand but because you have, quite sensibly, been selective in your choice – and that this particular vacancy meets all your criteria.

Make it clear that you have been proactive in your job hunt but that the right job isn't always available at the right time. You have consciously chosen not to leap into a new role simply in order to remain in employment.

You also need to be prepared for the interviewer to follow up by asking why you left your last job – assuming they haven't asked already.

Besides difficulty in finding work, other reasons for being out of the workplace include undertaking further training/education, raising a child, caring for another dependant, travel and ill health.

For further advice on how to handle these circumstances please take a look at Question 29, 'Why is there a gap in your CV?' in the previous chapter, Chapter 20, 'Fifty more classic questions: be prepared'.

Example:
Whilst it wouldn't have been difficult for me to find a job, I will admit that it hasn't been easy for me to find the right job. My career path is important to me and, given that I expect to remain in my next role for

a fair few years, I have felt it sensible to take a few months to explore various opportunities and make sure I am selecting one which is right for me. I plan my career carefully and it is important to me that the next step meets with my long-term career goals. I have been very selective but this particular vacancy certainly meets all my criteria.

14 What's your sickness record like?

Alternative and related questions:

- How many days did you take off sick last year and why?
- What would your current employer say if I asked them about your sickness record?
- How's your health?

The meaning behind the question:
Time is money or, more particularly, your time is your employer's money. No employer likes to lose money through staff being off sick. By directly questioning you on this topic the interviewer can gauge whether you are likely to be reliable in your attendance at work – or whether you might pose a liability.

Your answer:
It may well be tempting to give the interviewer a glowing account of your complete lack of illness. However, it is important to remember that the interviewer will most likely be seeking a reference from your last boss – and this is just the kind of fact that they may well check up on!

If you have been absent from work as a result of a significant illness or a major accident then you will have to disclose this – but do not be embarrassed or defensive about it. The interviewer should appreciate that these things do happen and, as long as they are not given any reason to suspect that you were 'faking it', you should have nothing at all to be worried about. And if they're not understanding about this then do you really want to work for them anyway? If the incident was recent then it's obviously important to emphasise that the issue is now completely resolved and you are fully fit for work.

Example:
Generally, I have a very good sickness record. I'm rarely off work as a result of illness. I was unfortunate last year to catch flu and also to suffer a bout of food poisoning. These both kept me off work for a few days – but only a few days. I'm fit and healthy and I recover quickly. A year can easily go by without my taking a single day off sick.

15 *What do you think of me as an interviewer?*

Alternative and related questions:

- Do you think I'm a good interviewer?

The meaning behind the question:
A strange question – and, in most cases, totally irrelevant to your ability to do the job for which you are applying! The interviewer has two aims here:

- To throw you off balance and see how you react under pressure

To see how you handle the social challenge of having to appraise somebody's performance – somebody who is ostensibly your superior.

Your answer:
While it's perfectly acceptable to visually express a little surprise at the question (you're only human, after all) you definitely don't want to lose your composure. It is essential to remain calm under fire. And it's not a difficult question really – the key is to strike a balance between being excessively critical and being excessively sycophantic whilst still communicating a meaningful observation.

> Example:
> Well, I would say you're doing a good job of assessing my specific ability to undertake this role as well as identifying what sort of person I am – what my character is, how I interact on a social level, what I'd be like to work with – and, with questions like this, you're doing a very good job of seeing how I react when I'm put on the spot!

16 *If you were in my position, what questions would you be asking?*

Alternative and related questions:

- If you were interviewing someone for this job what would you most like to ask them?

The meaning behind the question:
On the one hand, the interviewer is genuinely looking for a question (or questions) they haven't thought of and perhaps should have. On the other hand, in unexpectedly reversing your roles they are looking to see how well you can think on your feet.

Your answer:
You're going to need to give the interviewer a possible question – if not a couple of possible questions. There's no way you can answer along the lines of 'I think you've already asked everything that I would have asked.'

The only way in which this question might be tricky is if you're unprepared for it – which most candidates will be. Other than that, it's a gift horse – because it gives you the opportunity to deliver a positive and pre-prepared answer to a question of your choice.

It's all too easy to interpret this question as, 'What would be the toughest question I could ask you?' – and that is, of course, the last thing you should do. If you select your seven 'favourite' questions (or, more precisely, your seven favourite answers) from the previous chapter then it's unlikely that any one interviewer will ask you all seven. This should leave you with one or two up your sleeve to roll out on just this occasion.

Don't select from my 'Top 10' – because most of these will crop up in almost any interview.

I would naturally recommend you don't select from this chapter – with one exception. If you feel confident enough to pull it off then you could plump for 'What makes you better than any of the other candidates I'm interviewing?' (see Question 18 below). I would generally recommend you stick to safer ground though.

Example:
You've already asked many of the questions that I myself would be asking. I've obviously been to a few interviews in my time and, if I had to think of a question I would ask – that you haven't asked already – I think I would say, 'What have you learned and how have you developed over the last year/five years?'

17 *What would be the toughest question I could ask you?*

Alternative and related questions:

- What's the toughest question you've ever been asked at an interview?

The meaning behind the question:
This is a question which puts you firmly on the spot. Obviously, once the interviewer knows what the toughest question is they're going to be expecting your answer. As well as seeing how you react to stress, they will be hoping to identify a chink in your armour – the main reason you'd feel a question to be tough is, of course, because it hits a raw nerve and exposes a weakness.

Your answer:
There's no doubt about it – if you're not prepared for this question then this question itself is probably one of the toughest you're likely to ever get hit with. However, if you're prepared then it's a completely different kettle of fish.

It goes without saying that you should definitely not really tell them what the toughest question is. This is an opportunity to get the interviewer to ask you a question of your choice – one for which you know you can deliver a positive and impressive response.

You obviously need to suggest a question that can definitely be described as 'tough' – and, ideally, it should be a question an interviewer is unlikely to ask you. It makes sense to have three or four possibilities lined up just in case your 'favourite' has already cropped up earlier in the interview – and in case the interviewer follows up by asking you to pick another one! I'd suggest you simply pick out three or four of the tougher questions from the previous chapter.

Example:
I would say this question itself is probably one of the toughest you could ask me! Let me see ... I suppose that, for me, a really tough question would be one that exposes a weakness, something along the lines of 'What's the worst mistake you've made at work?'

18 What makes you better than any of the other candidates I'm interviewing?

Alternative and related questions:

- What would you say if I told you that you're not the best candidate I've seen so far?
- I don't think you've got what we need. Why should I hire you?
- If I told you that I don't think you're the candidate we're looking for, what would you say to try to change my mind?
- Do you really feel you're up to this job?

The meaning behind the question:
The interviewer may be indicating that you have failed to convince them so far that you are the best candidate for the job. Alternatively, they may just be asking you to pitch yourself. Either way, what is really being looked for is for you to give at least one good reason why you should be hired and not someone else.

Your answer:
As you can see under 'Alternative and related questions', there are many different ways in which the interviewer can ask you this question. Regardless of the actual words they use, you should aim to answer the question as if you had been asked, 'If I told you that I don't think you're the candidate we're looking for, what would you say to try to change my mind?'

To answer this question successfully you need to have a clear understanding of what the perfect candidate for the job would be and how best you match that description – more so than the other candidates. But don't go overboard in your answer; you probably don't know anything about the other candidates!

This sort of question generally comes towards the end of an interview so if you feel that the interviewer's previous questions have failed to cover one of your major selling points then now is the time to speak up or forever hold your peace.

Example:
I couldn't comment on other candidates for the job but I can say that, having now been working in this industry for over a decade, I have built up a very enviable network of contacts which I think most other candidates would find hard to beat. I have developed successful relationships with key decision-makers in numerous companies and this enables me to achieve a sales conversion rate much higher than average. I believe that my previous track record is clear evidence of what I would be able to achieve for you if you decided to appoint me to the role. I'm ambitious, highly driven and I relish a challenge.

19 I think you're overqualified for this job. Don't you?

Alternative and related questions:

- What would you say if I told you I thought you were overqualified for this job?

The meaning behind the question:
In asking this question, the interviewer has most likely already concluded that you are, technically, overqualified for the job. By asking this question, they're giving you a chance to comment on the matter – to explain to them why it is that you want this job when it is seemingly 'beneath' you.

Being overqualified for a position is a significant hurdle, as employing such an individual can – unless you can justify yourself – pose a major risk to the interviewer. Are you desperate and prepared to take any job going whether you are really interested in it or not? Are you going to be disappointed with the role and move on quickly? Are you going to cause problems in the hierarchy?

Your answer:
If you are overqualified for the position then you're going to need to address the issue. There are a number of reasons why you would be considering a job for which you are theoretically overqualified – not least a

challenging economic climate with high unemployment and a scarcity of jobs. Regardless of what your actual reasons are, you need to deliver a very convincing explanation to the interviewer if your application is to survive this question.

Naturally, if you don't feel you're overqualified then do query this with the interviewer. If they can tell you why they think you're overqualified, then it will help you to counter any objections. But perhaps you have simply misunderstood what the role entails and this vacancy isn't appropriate for you?

> Example:
> I realise that my last position was a management role – and I certainly found that experience invaluable. However, I have concluded that what I really want to do is work directly with clients, finding solutions to their needs and subsequently delivering and implementing those solutions. I don't see this as taking a step down the ladder; it's purely a question of my seeking out a role to which I am best suited, which I will enjoy and to which I will consequently be able to give my all. I believe my previous management experience will undoubtedly be very useful in terms of my being better able to understand the bigger picture. However, I am definitely happier and more productive in a customer-facing role.

20 What will you do if I decide not to hire you?

Alternative and related questions:

- What effect would it have on you if we decided not to hire you?
- How would you feel if your application for this job was unsuccessful?

The meaning behind the question:
No, this doesn't necessarily mean the interviewer is going to turn you down. It's yet another stress question. The interviewer will also be interested in seeing how you handle rejection and what your other job search plans are.

Your answer:
As with many seemingly negative questions, this is an opportunity for you to make a positive statement confirming your interest in the role – but making it clear that you're by no means desperate and know you will be in demand elsewhere. Don't react defensively or aggressively. Keep your cool and answer the question in a very matter-of-fact manner.

Example:
I would naturally be disappointed. I'm very keen to get this job. It meets all my requirements and I firmly believe that I also meet all your requirements. Yours is an organisation I can certainly see myself working well for. However, I do of course have a number of other applications in progress for similar roles and, if my application for this job was not successful, I would clearly continue to pursue other opportunities. But this particular role does remain my preferred choice and I hope I have demonstrated that I would be an ideal candidate for the job.

21 See this pen? Can you sell it to me?

Alternative and related questions:

- See this pen/pencil/paperclip/computer/desk/mobile phone/shoe ...

The meaning behind the question:
You might think this question is only likely to be asked if you work in sales – but you'd be wrong. It can be asked of almost anyone, regardless of whether sales skills are important to the job. It's a question which forces candidates to think on their feet while under pressure – and this can tell an interviewer a lot about candidate, not least how clearly they are able to think and communicate. It's a classic question – some might say cliché – but it nonetheless regularly features in interviews.

Your answer:
There are two possible ways of answering this question – depending on your line of work. If you do work in sales then you shouldn't need too much advice from me as to how to handle the question. You simply need to demonstrate your standard sales patter and techniques to the interviewer, inventing pricing, discount offers, payment terms, etc. as you go. The precise details are not important; it's the methods you employ which count – identifying the customer's needs and matching those to the specific benefits of the product, etc.

If, on the other hand, you don't work in sales (which is the majority of us) then this question is going to be a little trickier to handle. Don't let yourself be panicked though; the interviewer knows full well that you are not used to selling and won't be expecting you to have a whole arsenal of sales techniques at your disposal. And don't take yourself too seriously; good people are always light-hearted and friendly.

Concentrate on:

- Talking the interviewer into expressing a need – or needs.

- Describing the object, including both its features and, more importantly, its benefits.
- Discussing pricing (which you will invent off the top of your head).
- Asking the interviewer directly for the sale.

Example:
I'm sure you'll agree with me that a pen is vital to your day-to-day work and it's therefore important to make sure you've got just the right one. This pen is solidly constructed so as to be durable for everyday use – even if it rolls off your desk onto the floor. It has a plentiful ink reserve so there's less chance of the pen running dry at a critical moment. It fits comfortably into the hand and even has a clip so you can safely attach it to your jacket pocket when you're on the move. I can offer you this pen at the very reasonable price of 20 pence. However, if you were to take three – I'm sure your colleagues would also be interested – then I could offer you a 20 per cent discount making a total of just 48 pence. How many would you like?

Word of warning: this is a question where (unless you work in sales) it is particularly important to convince the interviewer that your answer is not rehearsed. If they can clearly identify that you have planned, prepared and rehearsed for this question then it's going to take a whole lot of impact out of your answer.

22 If you were an animal at the zoo, which animal would you be and why?

Alternative and related questions:

- If you were a dog, what breed of dog would you be?
- If you were a biscuit, what type of biscuit would you be?
- If you were a make of car, what make would you be?
- If you were a fruit, what fruit would you be?

The meaning behind the question:
Clearly the interviewer fancies themselves as a bit of an amateur psychiatrist. Superficially, it's a fairly silly question. However, the answers candidates give can be very revealing. The interviewer is obviously testing your ability to think on your feet – but is also looking for some further insight into how you perceive yourself.

Your answer:
This is definitely one of the most difficult questions to answer. You've got to quickly think of all the different possible animals (or dog breeds or cars,

etc.) and then pick one which has certain – positive – characteristics which you feel match your own. You've then got to explain your choice to the interviewer. This isn't easy – but don't panic; stall for time if necessary. And remember that there is no 'correct' answer to the question – it's all about how you reach your answer and how you express yourself.

Example:
I can't say anyone has ever asked me that before! If I could just have a second to think about it ... Right, I think the chimpanzee springs to my mind. They're a lot like humans really. They work together as a team, cooperate with each other for the benefit of the whole group, are sensitive to each other socially – and they always seem to have a good sense of fun and humour!

23 *If there was a monkey hanging from a chandelier, how would you get it down?*

Alternative and related questions:

- If there was a venomous snake sunbathing on your patio how would you get rid of it?

The meaning behind the question:
We're clearly getting into the weird and wacky with this question – but interviewers have been known to ask such questions. You might think you'll never get asked such a seemingly ridiculous question in an interview. However, I can personally vouch that questions like this do get asked – having been asked precisely this question myself many years ago!

Your answer:
There is no 'right' answer to this sort of question. It is purely a test of your ability to analyse a problem and identify possible solutions. Once you realise this you will hopefully be a lot less rattled by the question than I was at what was virtually my first ever interview! Don't let yourself be rattled by the question – and don't lose your sense of humour either. However, telling the interviewer you'd probably get your rifle out is unlikely to go down well!

Example:
Interesting question! I suppose there are a number of possible solutions to this problem. It's a case of identifying these possible solutions and selecting the one which has the best chance of success. The most obvious idea which springs to my mind is to try to entice it down by offering it, for example, a banana. Alternatively, I could try to scare it down. Shouting at it would probably make it even less likely to come

down, but flicking the light switch on and off might work. Spraying water at it might also convince it to budge but there's perhaps too much risk of collateral damage. Failing that, I think I'd find the monkey's owner or keeper and I'd delegate the task to them!

24 Why don't polar bears eat penguins?

Alternative and related questions:

- Why do butterflies generally come out during the day and moths generally come out at night?

The meaning behind the question:
You might think this question is along the same lines as Question 23, 'If there was a monkey hanging from a chandelier, how would you get it down?' However, technically, this is actually a general knowledge question. Polar bears don't eat penguins because polar bears live in the Arctic and penguins live in the Antarctic – a very long way away! However, in asking this sort of question, the interviewer doesn't really expect many people to get the right answer – and doesn't necessarily care too much if they do. They are more interested in how you think your answer through – so, yes, unless you know the 'correct' answer, this question is indeed similar to the previous question.

Your answer:
'Because they can't get the wrappers off.'? Well, that would certainly be one possible answer. Let's face it you're probably not a zoologist and this is one occasion where demonstrating a sense of humour – not to mention some lateral thinking – wouldn't do you any harm. I certainly know of at least one candidate who answered in this fashion. However, assuming you don't know the correct answer nor are you a budding comedian, the best answer to give is along the same lines as the previous question – demonstrate your ability to analyse the situation and identify possible theories.

> Example:
> I'm afraid I'll have to admit that biology isn't one of my strong points! I do enjoy watching documentaries but I haven't seen one yet which would give me the answer to this question. I can think of a number of possible hypotheses – maybe penguins are too small for a polar bear to bother with and they stick to larger prey, maybe polar bears aren't fast enough to catch a penguin, perhaps there's something toxic about penguins – some form of defence mechanism, maybe polar bears live and hunt inland but penguins spend most of their time in the water or at the water's edge. I obviously don't know for sure – but these would be my possible ideas. Am I close?

25 *How much water would it take to fill St Paul's Cathedral?*

Alternative and related questions:

- How many bottles of red wine are drunk in France on Christmas Day?

The meaning behind the question:
This is definitely not a general knowledge question! It is a question specifically designed to test your reasoning skills. The interviewer wants to see how you approach the problem, how able you are to identify the relevant factors and, having identified the relevant factors, how you use them to calculate your answer. They are not expecting you to be able to give a precise figure. They are mainly looking to see how you rise to the challenge of attempting to formulate an answer.

Your answer:
You'd be forgiven for pausing for a second to think your answer through. This is most definitely not an easy question! Try to keep a clear head and identify what factors will lead you to an answer. You're not expected to be an expert on St Paul's Cathedral – nor on French wine-drinking habits. The key is to try to think through the question logically and to convey your thoughts to the interviewer in an ordered fashion.

> Example:
> That's a difficult question! If we assume that we have already plugged up any potential leaks then the answer primarily hinges on a precise calculation of the internal volume of St Paul's Cathedral. I don't know St Paul's Cathedral very well but I know it's a complicated piece of architecture. In order to answer the question reasonably precisely I'd need to see plans of the building so that I could break it up into a number of different shapes, measure them and calculate their volumes accordingly. I'd also have to make a deduction for interior furniture, etc. although I would expect that to be fairly minor.

If your work involves having to handle complex calculations of this nature then you might want to take your answer to the next level by actually having a stab at the correct figure.

> Example:
> At a guess, I'd say St Paul's is roughly 200m long, 50m wide and 50m high – making a total of half a million cubic metres. Features such as the dome will add to this figure but, likewise, internal furnishings, pillars and walls will reduce it. With 1,000 litres in a cubic metre, half a million cubic metres equates to 500 million litres. Without more precise data that would be my best estimate. Seeing the plans of the

building would be useful but another technique would be to buy a scale model from a souvenir shop or suchlike. I could then determine an upper limit by plugging any leaks, placing it in water, measuring how much water it displaced and then scaling this figure up.

Word of warning:

Having answered such questions, don't make the mistake of asking what the correct answer is. The interviewer probably won't know and you might just make them feel a little foolish!

Chapter **22**

Illegal questions – and how to dodge them

While it is clear from the previous few chapters that interviewers might question you on a whole range of different subjects, you need to know that they do not have the right to ask you anything they please. There are a number of topics which the law specifically prohibits them from discussing.

The main reason an interviewer will ask such questions is that they are lacking in experience. An HR professional will be well aware of the rules and generally steer clear of such questions. An owner-manager of a small company, on the other hand, might very well be blissfully ignorant that it is illegal to ask such a seemingly innocent question as 'Do you have children?'

If there wasn't the possibility that you might get asked illegal questions then I wouldn't have bothered writing this chapter. However, I regret that it is a fact of life that many interviewers will still ask such questions and I therefore need to equip you to handle them appropriately.

Effectively handling illegal questions can be tough.

Why are certain questions illegal?

While most questions that an interviewer asks are designed to help discriminate between different candidates, they should be discriminating on the grounds of your ability to do the job. They should not be discriminating on one of a number of different grounds which are deemed to be unfairly discriminatory – unfairly discriminatory because they are not relevant to your ability to undertake the role for which you are applying.

What should you do when confronted with an illegal question?

Answering an illegal question is going to be a real test of your diplomatic abilities.

First of all, you face the problem that, depending on how they have phrased their question, it might be hard to establish whether it really is an illegal question or just an inappropriate personal question.

Assuming it is definitely an illegal question, if you point this out to the interviewer – that they shouldn't have asked it and that you have no intention of answering it – then I can virtually guarantee that it's going to destroy your chances of getting the job. This is especially so if the interviewer was totally unaware that it was an illegal question – which will generally be the case.

Whilst I have the utmost respect for the laws which attempt to protect candidates from discrimination, in practice the best solution is going to be for you to answer the question but to aim to sidestep it and steer the conversation away from this particular topic.

TOP TIP

Be aware that, just because an interviewer has asked you a potentially discriminatory question, it doesn't necessarily follow that they are prejudiced in any way. It may simply have been a poor choice of question. It is therefore important not to take it personally and consequently react in a hostile manner. The interviewer may have betrayed a certain lack of professionalism; don't allow yourself to follow their example.

What types of illegal question might you have to face?

There are a whole host of possible questions you might be asked which will, to one degree or another, fit the definition of 'illegal'. However, they can be broken down into a small number of key areas – age discrimination, sexual discrimination, racial discrimination, religious discrimination, disability discrimination, discrimination on the grounds of trade union membership and, finally, discrimination on the basis of 'spent' criminal convictions.

I will cover each of these in turn below.

Age discrimination

An interviewer could ask, 'How old are you?' – which you might think is a reasonably harmless question, although possibly a little personal. Alternatively, they might elaborate on the question in such a way as to reveal why questioning you on your age is simply not acceptable:

- Aren't you a little young to hold a position of this level?
- Aren't you perhaps a little old to cope with this job?

These questions might very well make you feel rather more uncomfortable.

Are they discriminatory?

Are you indeed too young to be able to have a position of such responsibility/authority? Or are you too old to keep up with such a fast-paced role?

Of course not ...

William Pitt was just 24 when he became Great Britain's youngest Prime Minister. He went on to spend a total of 20 years in office during the course of a highly distinguished career.

William Gladstone, on the other hand, was still going strong as British Prime Minister at the age of 84.

I will admit that these are fairly extreme examples but being Prime Minister of Great Britain is a fairly extreme job and, whether 24 years old or 84 years old, both these individuals succeeded admirably.

The Employment Equality (Age) Regulations 2006 make it quite clear that an interviewer should not be questioning you on your age. You should no longer even put your date of birth on your CV.

While an interviewer has the right to make their selection on the basis of experience – which may sometimes favour more mature candidates – they should not rule someone out of the recruitment process on the basis of age.

If you're faced with a question concerning your age, phrase your answer in such a way as to demonstrate to the interviewer that your age is not a relevant factor; it is your skills and experience that count. Use this question as an opportunity to reiterate your key selling points and how they match the requirements of the job.

I would note that legislation is always complicated and I have, of necessity, simplified the interpretations given in this chapter. You should be aware that there are always exceptions to every rule. For example, if you are older than – or within six months of – an employer's normal retirement age then an employer does have the right to reject your application on these grounds. However, most exceptions are fairly minor and will only apply to a very small percentage of individuals.

Sexual discrimination

Whilst it is normally very clear when a question is discriminatory on the grounds of age, sexual discrimination can be a lot less obvious.

Sexual discrimination is normally a greater problem for female applicants; however it is important to be aware that male applicants can also be targeted. It all depends on the circumstances and the precise line of questioning that an interviewer adopts.

'Are you married?' might seem an innocuous enough question to ask either a man or a woman – and it's not actually illegal for an interviewer to ask this. However, it can rapidly lead on to a whole gamut of questions which contravene the Sex Discrimination Act:

- Do you have any children?
- Do you plan to have any children?
- When do you plan to have children?
- You're not pregnant, are you?

Previously, many candidates would volunteer information about their family on their CV:

Marital status: *Married; two children*

However, this is now considered a potential invitation to discriminate and it is definitely no longer recommended.

Once an interviewer has established your marital status and whether or not you have children, it may lead them into severely discriminatory territory:

- What impact will the travel requirements of this job have on your family?
- How does your wife/girlfriend/husband/boyfriend feel about you taking this job?
- Is arranging childcare going to cause problems for you?

Your marital status is not relevant to your ability to do the job. Your family is your own private business. What impact this job might have on members of your family and whether taking this job might cause you any problems are issues that you will have to deal with; they have nothing to do with your employer and they don't have any right to be questioning you on such subjects.

When faced with such questions, it's probably not going to be to your advantage to take offence. Try to handle such questions in a very matter-of-fact manner and, if you can identify your interviewer's concerns, you may wish to address these – but make sure you don't come across as being defensive. The interviewer shouldn't have asked you the question in the first place so you hold the moral high ground.

Besides questions relating to your marital status and your children, it is worth mentioning that there are a variety of other lines of questioning which are deemed to constitute sexual discrimination, including questions regarding your sexual orientation. While these are less likely to crop up in interviews, it has been known.

Racial discrimination

It's important to note that racial discrimination isn't limited to the colour of your skin. Racial discrimination can be a whole lot more subtle than that; it could come down to a simple difference of nationality – or even the town or county in which you were born.

However, it is usually pretty obvious whether or not a question is racially discriminatory:

- Where were you born?
- Where do you come from?
- What is your mother tongue?

These types of questions are normally totally irrelevant and are consequently discriminatory.

While an employer has the right to ensure that you are entitled to work in the UK and is allowed to select on the basis of your ability to communicate in English (or any other language, for that matter) they are not allowed to discriminate arbitrarily on the basis of your geographic or ethnic origins.

Racial discrimination is one of the most widespread and pervasive forms of discrimination – and many readers of this book will be painfully aware of that fact.

STATISTIC

A recent BBC investigation revealed that 25 out of 30 recruiters agreed to a request to only send white applicants for a receptionist job. While the job in this case was hypothetical, prejudiced employers most certainly exist and you may well find yourself confronted with one.

My advice would be to answer any such questions in a factually correct fashion – and to say no more. This isn't a topic you should dwell on.

As I have previously mentioned, the interviewer is not necessarily prejudiced. They might just be curious (and inexperienced).

If, however, you suspect the interviewer is prejudiced in some way then you need to ask yourself:

- Would you really want to work with/for such an individual?
- Would you be prepared to take the matter further and make a formal complaint?

These are questions that only you can answer. Personally, I feel that, while it may be in your own best interests to let the matter drop, this world needs people to stand up to such behaviour if we are ever to succeed in eradicating it completely.

Religious discrimination

Discrimination on religious grounds is rare. While religious differences continue to be the cause of conflict, we nevertheless live in an increasingly secular society.

Interviewers are unlikely to question you as to your religious beliefs, largely because the issue is unlikely to cross their minds. The most likely reason for the idea to pop into their heads is if some aspect of your appearance outwardly reveals your beliefs, for example you might wear a Star of David on your necklace. Religious discrimination is also closely linked with racial discrimination and, if an interviewer has identified a racial difference between you, they may also suspect a religious difference.

The bottom line is that this question is (in almost all cases) completely and utterly irrelevant. It's absolutely none of the interviewer's business.

There is, however, nothing to be gained by getting indignant. My advice would be the same as for a racially focused question – answer factually but don't elaborate. The interviewer will hopefully move swiftly on to other, more appropriate, topics.

Disability discrimination

It is permissible for an employer to question you as to whether or not you have a disability. However, the Disability Discrimination Act generally prevents them from taking a disability into account when making their selection. On this basis, one might wonder why they have the right to ask you at interview and why it can't wait until a firm job offer has been made. The reason is that an employer is only obliged to make 'reasonable adjustments' to accommodate a disabled person. If, despite such adjustments, a candidate would still be unable to do the job effectively (as a result of their disability) then the employer is nonetheless allowed to reject the application.

There are various ways in which an interviewer could approach this topic:

- Do you have a disability?
- How do you cope with your disability?
- Can you undertake this job with your disability?
- What adjustments would we need to make to accommodate your disability?

However they go about questioning you, your aim should be to briefly disclose the nature of your disability and then go on to detail the adjustments which would be required for you to undertake the role.

While it is uncommon for an employer to discriminate on the basis of a disability itself, the interviewer may have concerns as to the changes that will need to be made. If you are aware of state funding which may be available to support such changes, then you can go a long way towards allaying such fears. You should also reassure them that, subject to these changes, you will be able to undertake the role just as effectively as a non-disabled person.

Trade union membership

Discrimination on the grounds of trade union membership can swing both ways. You could be discriminated against for being a member – and you could be discriminated against for *not* being a member.

Your membership (or lack of membership) of a trade union is not relevant to your ability to perform the job for which you are applying. Any questions on this topic are therefore inherently illegal.

You will be the best judge of how to answer any such questions. It will depend on your individual circumstances. You may feel it is to your advantage to disclose the truth. Alternatively, you may feel it is best to politely decline to answer. Being able to tell the truth is definitely preferable – but not if you think it's going to cost you the job.

Criminal convictions

The law does not currently provide a great deal of protection for those with criminal convictions. While some might feel that such individuals don't deserve any protection, this is a very short-sighted attitude. Failure to rehabilitate offenders by helping them to reintegrate into society will inevitably lead to higher rates of recidivism.

Limited protection is afforded by the Rehabilitation of Offenders Act which allows for certain criminal convictions to be deemed 'spent' after what is termed a 'rehabilitation period'. If a criminal conviction is spent then you are permitted to conceal it from a prospective employer – with certain exceptions – and if you have any criminal convictions then it is vital to be aware of what this rehabilitation period is. The Act also makes it unlawful for record-keeping bodies such as the Criminal Records Bureau to disclose details of such convictions.

However, these general rules do not apply to certain employers and organisations. The rationale is to ensure that employers and organisations offering certain sensitive positions, professions and licences can access an applicant's full criminal history before reaching a decision.

If you are in any doubt as regards your own specific circumstances then it's always advisable to seek appropriate professional advice.

If you have convictions which aren't yet spent then you are legally obliged to disclose them *if asked* and, as the law stands, a recruiter is not formally prohibited from taking this into account when making a selection.

BLOOPER!

Upon being asked if they had a criminal record, one candidate replied, 'Yes, "Light My Fire" by Will Young!'

Exceptions to the rules: genuine occupational requirements

While there is plenty of legislation intended to prohibit unfair discrimination, I have already made it clear that there are certainly exceptions to the rules.

The most significant of these exceptions is where a 'genuine occupational requirement' (GOR) exists.

In cases where an individual's age, gender, sexual orientation, race or religion is genuinely required for them to be able to effectively perform a role, then an employer is permitted to claim a GOR and discriminate on one or more of these grounds – with the onus being on the employer to demonstrate that the personal characteristic concerned is indeed vital to the role.

For example, whilst your gender should normally be irrelevant to your ability to do your job, it would of course not be unreasonable for an employer looking for someone to work in a female-only spa to request that only female candidates apply for the role. To cite another example, a halal butcher must of course be a Muslim.

Chapter **23**

Special cases: from school leavers to retirees

The questions an interviewer chooses to ask you will of course depend on numerous factors – one of those factors being what stage of your career you have reached.

Regardless of your circumstances, the majority of the questions I've covered in this book should be relevant to you. However, there are a few specific cases I'd like to handle in this chapter – both because they are likely to encompass a significant proportion of my readers and because, if you fall into one of these categories, you might be faced with certain specific questions for which you need to be prepared – or subtle variations on questions we've already covered:

- school leavers
- recent graduates
- changing career path
- returning to work after a career break
- retirees and those approaching retirement

As always, forewarned is forearmed!

School leavers

If you're a recent school leaver then you definitely qualify as a special case – primarily because you will have little or possibly no previous work experience. You may think this rules out quite a number of the classic questions interviewers like to pose. However, skilled interviewers will normally be able to rephrase their questions so as to probe not your work experience but your school record.

'How would your colleagues describe you?' can be turned into 'How would your teachers describe you?'

By switching one word, 'Can you tell me about a major problem at work that you've had to deal with?' becomes 'Can you tell me about a major problem at school that you've had to deal with?'

And 'Can you tell me about the best boss you've ever had?' translates easily to 'Can you tell me about your favourite teacher?'

While these types of questions need a little adaptation, you will find that many of the classic questions can just as easily apply to school life as they can to working life:

- Do you work well on your own initiative?
- How do you handle pressure and stress?
- Can you tell me about a time when you have failed to achieve a goal?

There are also a number of questions which are only ever likely to be asked of a recent school leaver:

- What subjects did you most enjoy at school?
- What subjects did you least enjoy?
- How were your final exams?
- What did you normally do during the school holidays?
- Why haven't you decided to continue your education?
- Wouldn't you like to go/shouldn't you have gone to university?

You need to be prepared for these and to have thought through and perfected your answers just as you would when preparing for any other interview question.

If you don't have any work experience then the interviewer will be aware of this and, if it was a major obstacle to your performing the job, they wouldn't be bothering to interview you. If they are taking the time to interview you then it's because they believe you may have something to offer – and you should draw on your school experiences to help make a compelling case that you do indeed have something to offer.

TOP TIP

Don't be shy. Speak up! And avoid giving monosyllabic 'Yes' and 'No' answers if it's at all possible – it nearly always is. Too many school leavers fail at interview because they are simply uncommunicative.

Recent graduates

Recent graduates are also a special case, not only because they are also likely to be lacking in practical work experience, but because they are very likely to be subjected to detailed questioning about their time at university.

As for school leavers, most of the standard interview questions can be adapted or rephrased to cope with the fact that you will have little or no work experience. You therefore need to be just as prepared for all the most common questions as any other candidate needs to be. You may have very little in the way of work experience so you will have to construct your answers in the light of your university experiences. This isn't a problem though – as a graduate you have a lot to offer an employer even if you don't yet have any relevant work experience. Is successfully completing a degree course really that different from 'working' life?

Besides the generic questions, there are of course many other questions specific to recent graduates that an interviewer may decide to pose.

In a previous chapter we covered the question, 'In what ways is your degree relevant to the work you are now doing?' This could be asked of someone who graduated a year ago – or ten years ago. However, for someone who has only just graduated, an interviewer will probably rephrase this along the lines of 'In what ways is your degree relevant to your ability to do this job?' It's vital to give careful thought to your answer in advance – because this one is a favourite among interviewers.

Other popular questions for graduates include:

- Why did you decide to go to this university?
- Why did you decide to read this particular subject?
- What class of degree are you expecting/did you achieve?
- What aspects of going to university did you enjoy the most?
- Which module/course/project did you most enjoy?
- What extracurricular activities did you engage in?
- How has life at university prepared you for the workplace?

I can't answer these questions for you. It's up to you to apply the principles we have covered so far in this book so as to produce your own answers. But remember how important it is to bear in mind that the interviewer will be assessing your answers in the context of the job for which you are applying. Be positive in your answers – demonstrate the drive and enthusiasm which led you to the successful completion of your degree. Your lack of practical experience may be a small disadvantage – but your degree is a powerful selling point.

Changing career path

If you have decided to change your career path then the main obstacle you face will be your lack of relevant experience. You may have a wealth of experience in the workplace but, if it's not directly relevant to the job for which you are applying then this will certainly present you with a challenge.

TOP TIP

Make sure you highlight your willingness to learn new skills and to undertake additional training if necessary. Having the right attitude – enthusiastic and determined – is essential.

When formulating your answers you should ensure that your comments remain relevant – and try to focus on the transferable skills and abilities that you have developed.

Interviewers are always going to be curious about a candidate whose career hasn't followed a straight path. You can expect to be questioned on this in a variety of different ways:

- Why have you decided to change your career path?
- What difficulties do you perceive in changing your career path?
- How will you be able to compensate for your lack of relevant experience?
- What are your key transferable skills and abilities?
- Would you say that you're a quick learner?
- Why didn't you want to remain in your previous line of work?
- What makes you think this line of work will be right for you?

Returning to work after a career break

If you're returning to work after a career break – most commonly because you've taken time out to raise children – then this is always going to raise some questions in an interviewer's mind.

We have already discussed sexual discrimination in the previous chapter and established that an interviewer should not be asking you questions about your married life, your children or your future family plans. However, there will be no avoiding the fact that there is a large hole in your CV which you will be expected to account for (and should already have accounted for within your CV). You may also be affected by other prejudices, most notabley ageism.

The main question the interviewer will be asking themself is why they should be hiring you, rather than someone who is perhaps younger and possesses more recent qualifications and experience. I'm not saying this is fair; I'm simply saying it's important to know that this is what they're thinking – because it will help you when phrasing your answers (and even when writing your CV) to know what you're up against.

They may also be worried about the possibility that your family commitments will have a detrimental effect on your work:

- Will working overtime be a problem for your family?
- Is it going to be difficult for your family if you have to travel?
- How reliable are your childcare arrangements?

They're not really permitted to ask you such questions but, again, you need to keep in mind that this is what they will be thinking and that these are the sorts of objections you are going to need to overcome. By identifying your interviewer's concerns, you are better able to find ways to address these – but make sure you don't come across as being defensive.

Questions they are more likely to ask – and for which you need to be prepared – include:

- Why have you decided now is the right time to return to the workplace?
- Are you sure a full-time role is the right choice for you?
- How do you think the industry/sector has changed since you were last in work?

Of course, there are many other reasons for a career break, including:

- further training/education
- caring for a family member or close friend
- travel
- inability to find a suitable position
- ill health
- imprisonment.

For the full story on how to handle these circumstances, please take a look at Question 29, 'Why is there a gap in your CV?' in Chapter 20, 'Fifty more classic questions: be prepared'.

Retirees and those approaching retirement

We discussed age discrimination in the previous chapter and established that it is totally unacceptable for interviewers to ask, 'How old are you?'

However, this isn't necessarily going to stop them thinking along the lines of:

- Aren't you perhaps a little old to cope with this job?
- Are you too old to keep up with such a fast-paced role?

They're certainly not allowed to ask such questions but they may hit you with a variety of other questions which you need to be prepared to handle:

- Have you given any thought to your retirement plans?
- At what age are you planning to retire?
- Why have you decided to work on past normal retirement age?

The important thing for you to bear in mind is that your age is not a relevant factor; it is your skills and experience that count. Demonstrate these effectively to the interviewer and the 'age factor' will hopefully be forgotten.

Chapter 24

Yet more questions

Whilst I have covered all the most frequently asked interview questions in this book, there are of course many other possible questions you could be asked.

It is beyond the scope of this book to analyse hundreds more questions in detail but I would like to list some of the more important ones – for you to read through, think about and draft your own rough answers to.

Once you are familiar with an interview question you can never again be stumped or surprised by it – and being surprised in an interview is the last thing you want to happen. Surprise leads to pressure, pressure leads to stress, stress leads to panic – and panic can ruin your interview very quickly!

Some of these questions will, to a degree, be variations on the same theme as one or more of the questions I have already covered and it is up to you to think them through and adapt your pre-prepared answers to fit the circumstances.

Other questions will be completely new to you and, while you are less likely to be asked them, it never hurts to be prepared.

Talking about your current employment

- Can you tell me what you enjoy about your current job?
- What will you remember most about your last job?
- Is this the first time you have made an effort to move away from your current employer?
- How do you feel about the possibility of leaving your current job?
- How would you describe your current employer?

Talking about this vacancy

- Wouldn't you be better suited to working in a larger/smaller organisation?
- How do you feel this vacancy differs from your current role?
- What reservations do you have about your ability to undertake this job?
- Can you describe your ideal working environment to me?
- How do you feel we compare to our competitors?
- What would you say is our unique selling point?
- What would be your analysis of the current trends in our industry/sector?

Understanding your career path, plans and ambitions

- What aspects of your career path would you like to have been different?
- What are your greatest regrets about the path your career has taken?
- What has been the greatest challenge you have faced in your career to date?
- What do you think are your main career options for the next five years?
- What exactly does the word 'success' mean to you?

Addressing problems in your career history

- Why did you stay with this organisation for such a short time?
- Why did you stay with this organisation for such a long time?

Coping with stress and pressure

- Are you able to multitask?
- Can you juggle a number of different projects simultaneously?
- How do you handle rejection/disappointment/failure?

Defining teamwork

- How do you deal with interpersonal conflict?
- What does tact and diplomacy mean to you?
- What makes for a successful team?

Management and leadership

- Would you describe yourself as a good manager?
- How would you describe your ideal team member?
- Do you really think you're management material?
- What is your attitude to delegation?
- Can you give me an example of a time when you had to lead from the front?
- Have you ever had to fire or lay off a member of your staff?

Personal and professional development

- In what ways do you intend to improve upon your performance?
- How has your current job prepared you for greater challenges/responsibility?

Interests and activities

- What book are you reading at the moment?
- What newspaper do you take?
- Are you interested in current affairs?

The amateur psychiatrist

- If you won the Lottery what would you do?
- Can you tell me about the best teacher you ever had?
- If you could meet any historical figure, who would it be and why?
- What are you most afraid of?

Money, money, money

- Why aren't you earning more?
- How much do you think you are really worth?
- How much does money matter to you?
- Would you still be interested in this job if your current employer offered a pay rise?
- Have you ever had to take a pay cut to keep your job?
- Have you ever asked for but been refused a pay rise?

Health

- Do you have any medical conditions to declare?

Relocation

- Why do you want to relocate?
- Can you perceive any problems in relocating?

Deal-making

- How would you react if I were to offer you this job on the spot?

Further help

While it is definitely beyond the scope of this book to cover the questions above in detail, I have covered them all on our website for you:

WEB LINK http://www.ineedacv.co.uk/yetmorequestions

However, I would reiterate the importance of taking the time to think through and create your own answers. This is definitely the very best way to prepare.

Chapter **25**

Ending the interview: your own questions

Interviews are always a two-way process. Not preparing your own questions for the end of an interview is therefore a common – and significant – interview mistake.

There aren't many interviews that conclude without the candidate being asked, 'Do you have any questions for me/us?' Almost all interviewers will give you a chance to ask questions and you should use this as an opportunity to further demonstrate your interest and enthusiasm. If you don't then you'll come across as passive and uninterested.

STATISTIC

A recent survey showed that 29 per cent of recruiters, when questioned, stated that the candidate not asking questions – or asking poor questions – at the end of the interview was sufficient reason for them to 'fail' them.

What to ask

Don't ask too many questions – you're the interviewee, not the interviewer – but do be prepared with a few intelligent questions, e.g. questions about their expectations, training, people you will be working with, the future, etc.

Here are some examples you might like to adapt to suit your own circumstances:

- What are the top priorities for my first six months in the job?
- How would you describe the team I will be working with?
- How do you see my role evolving over the next two to three years?
- How do you see the organisation evolving over the next five years?
- What training and professional development opportunities will be available?

You will notice that I have phrased these questions as if you had already bagged the job. It's a subtle psychological technique which will project self-confidence and help further persuade the interviewer that you are the right candidate for the job.

One last sales pitch

If you have not been asked about something which you feel illustrates an important aspect of your ability to do the job, don't be afraid to bring it up yourself at the end of the interview. You could, for example, ask how important such-and-such an ability is to the job. When the interviewer answers that it is indeed important then they've given you the perfect opportunity to roll out a pre-prepared example demonstrating that you have this ability.

An 'advanced' technique ...

Another good question to ask is whether or not the interviewer has any reservations about your application – and what they are. It takes a bit of nerve to ask this question and you had better make jolly sure you are ready to address any reservations they may have; this will probably be your last chance to do so. It might be described as an 'advanced' technique but if you can uncover any possible objections the interviewer might have to hiring you – and counter-attack effectively – then it can make all the difference. It's a question which will certainly demonstrate confidence in yourself at the very least.

STATISTIC

Don't ask questions just for the sake of it. One candidate, when asked if she had any questions, replied, 'Are you going anywhere nice on your holidays this summer?' Clearly that didn't make the best of impressions!

Topics to avoid

First of all, avoid questions which the interviewer may expect you to already have the answers to. This includes questions about the organisation which a quick look at their website could have answered. You'll expose a lack of preparation.

It's also best to avoid questions about pay and holidays – unless of course the interviewer brings up these topics themself. Such matters can always be covered in later discussions. Bringing them up during your interview can place too much focus on what you are expecting from the employer – rather than what you are offering them. This is never a good idea.

You should also avoid asking questions which the interviewer is unlikely to know the answers to! They won't take kindly to this at all. Your interviewer may well work within a centralised HR department – whose staff can't be expected to know the precise operational details of every other department.

TOP TIP

Whatever questions you select, be aware that they can reveal a lot about you – the way you think, your motivations, your needs, etc. Remember this and try to keep your questions upbeat and positive.

Wrapping up

In wrapping up, make sure that you find out when you can expect to hear whether or not you have been successful – it could be anything from the same day (in which case, you may be even asked to wait around for a decision) to a couple of weeks. Don't – ever – be tempted to ask the interviewer if they felt the interview went well – it smacks of desperation! I heard of one candidate who even admitted to the interviewer that he didn't feel the interview had gone very well and asked if perhaps there were any other jobs going elsewhere in the organisation! Don't let nerves get the better of you.

And, finally, remember to thank the interviewer for their time before you leave.

Summary

- Try to understand the meaning behind each question. Why have you been asked this question? What is it the interviewer is trying to find out?

- It is vitally important for you to think through and create your own answers to potential interview questions.
- There are no universally 'right' answers to interview questions – just answers that are right for *you*.
- Flagging up specific, relevant, real-life examples from your own experience is an ideal way of reinforcing your points in the interviewer's mind.
- Almost all interviewers will give you a chance to ask questions and you should use this as an opportunity to further demonstrate your interest and enthusiasm.

PART 4

THE 15 MOST COMMON INTERVIEW MISTAKES

Chapter **26**

How to avoid them!

The same common mistakes crop up time and time again at interview. Too many jobseekers miss out on their dream job because of a small number of easily avoided blunders.

Some of the mistakes that people make at interview are very obvious and others are more subtle. The CV Centre has conducted a comprehensive survey to derive a 'Top 15' and, in this chapter, I will list these 15 most common interview mistakes and refer you back to previous chapters, where necessary, to explain both why they are a mistake – and how to avoid them.

1 Not knowing enough about the job you're applying for

The key to preventing pre-interview jitters is to prepare yourself thoroughly. We fear what we don't know and what we can't control, yet there is so much you can do to plan and prepare for your interview – and the first item on your list should be to thoroughly research the job in question.

Not knowing the ins and outs of a job is among the worst blunders you can make in an interview – as is failing to demonstrate to the interviewer how you meet the requirements for the job.

If you are to be able to convince a recruiter that you are right for the role then you obviously need to first get it clear in your own mind why you are right for the role – and you can't do this unless you have properly researched and understood what it will involve.

For further guidance on researching for your job, please refer back to Chapter 1, 'Researching the job'.

2 Not knowing enough about the organisation you're applying to

A number of popular interview questions are designed to probe and assess your knowledge of the organisation to which you are applying. An interviewer will expect you to have done your homework. If you're unprepared and unable to answer these questions adequately then it's going to be a big black mark on your application.

Just as a lack of knowledge of the job in question will count against you, a lack of knowledge of the organisation will betray a lack of effort on your part.

How can they be sure you really want this job – and that you're really the right candidate for the job – if you know so little about their organisation?

BLOOPER!

One candidate, famously, upon being asked what they could bring to the company, responded with 'What is it that you do again?'

For further details on what to read up on before your interview, please refer back to Chapter 2, 'Researching the organisation'.

3 Arriving late

The importance of making appropriate travel arrangements to get to your interview may seem obvious. However, this is frequently a problem for candidates. Being late for an interview – even by only a few minutes – is a very common mistake but it will immediately count against you.

STATISTIC

Nearly half of recruiters won't give a candidate a job if they are more than ten minutes late for interview – regardless of how well they perform.

It's also important to arrive early in terms of allowing yourself time to relax and compose yourself.

For more advice on planning your travel arrangements, please see Chapter 3, 'Travel arrangements and safety considerations'.

4 Lacking enthusiasm

While there's obviously a fine balance here, enthusiasm in an interview is essential – just don't overdo it! Recruiters often find that the person they are interviewing lacks enthusiasm – and this will naturally count against you. Sometimes it might just be due to nerves and shyness – but don't let this happen to you. Be enthusiastic – and show it.

Confident people inspire confidence in others. If you appear confident that you are able to do the job, the employer is likely to be more inclined to believe that you can – and showing a lack of enthusiasm is generally fatal to your chances of success.

I talk about this subject in greater detail back in Chapter 4, 'Mental preparation'.

5 Arrogance

While confidence is critical to a successful interview, it is naturally important not to go to the other extreme and appear over confident or arrogant – which is a surprisingly common mistake. You simply need to appreciate what your strengths are and value yourself accordingly.

Issues such as nerves and confidence are covered in detail in Chapter 4, 'Mental preparation'.

6 Dressing inappropriately

Presentation, presentation, presentation.

The way you present yourself physically will make an impression on an interviewer before you even have a chance to open your mouth.

Present yourself professionally and the interviewer will see you as a professional – but the opposite also applies. Never forget that you are marketing yourself – and the way you present yourself can have an impact on the interviewer, almost as powerful as what you actually have to say for yourself.

Presentation can make all the difference between success and failure. Image is everything!

STATISTIC

Research has shown that your interviewer could well have made up their mind about you within just 30 seconds of having met you. Use this to your advantage.

While I'm not for one minute saying you're the sort of person who would wear white socks with their suit, if you're looking for advice on what to wear to your interview then take a look at Chapter 5, 'Presentation'.

7 Poor body language

Recruiters are trained to make informed assessments of candidates, based not only on how they communicate verbally but also on how they communicate physically.

Even if your interviewer has received no formal training, they are going to be inherently sensitive to certain nuances of body language – just like the rest of us. It's instinctive.

The importance of body language as a factor in the decision-making process should not be underestimated. Recruiters regularly complain about candidates' poor body language – limp handshake, lack of eye contact, slouching and failing to smile.

What's all this about body language? Take a look at Chapter 6, 'Body language'.

8 Poor first impressions

First impressions are extremely important. Interviewers can reach a decision about a candidate very quickly. Make a poor first impression and you might not be able to recover from it. How quickly do you sum up someone you've just met? It's probably less than a couple of minutes.

Remember: you never get a second chance to make a first impression.
Too many candidates turn up reeking of smoke or garlic – or worse!
How can you make a really strong first impression?

I help you to answer this question in Chapter 7, 'The Big Day' and Chapter 8, 'First impressions count'.

9 Answering the wrong question

It's actually surprisingly easy for your thoughts to stray elsewhere and for you to fail to listen properly to a question. You're in a stressful situation and you have a lot on your mind; it's perfectly possible to get distracted.

Interviewers often have to deal with candidates going off at a tangent and giving the answer to a totally different question than the one that was asked!

Listen – and engage your brain before opening your mouth!

I talk more about the basic principles of handling interview questions in Chapter 18, 'Basic principles'.

10 Failing to sell yourself effectively

Far too many candidates fail to sell themselves effectively at interview – giving boring, monosyllabic answers unsupported by any real-life examples.

It's essential for you to think through and create your own answers to potential questions. Wherever possible, try to integrate real-life examples into your answers rather than just speaking hypothetically. Flagging up specific, relevant examples from your own experience is an ideal way of reinforcing your points in the interviewer's mind.

More about this in Chapter 18, 'Basic principles'.

11 Being a parrot

So many candidates at interview make the mistake of sounding as if they're reciting from some old-fashioned book on interview technique with a title such as *1001 Interview Questions*!

Make sure you don't fall into this trap yourself. This is really important. There are no universally 'right' answers to interview questions – just answers that are right for *you*.

And even if you have prepared and memorised your own answers, you should be careful to make sure that your delivery is natural and doesn't come across as rehearsed.

This important topic is discussed in greater detail in Chapter 18, 'Basic principles'.

12 Lying

Never lie at interview or say something that you cannot substantiate.

For many candidates their troubles start even before they've been invited for the interview because a large percentage of people seem to think it's permissible to tell a few small porkies when writing their CV. Many think it's acceptable because 'everyone else does it' – and it is a fact that many prospective employers do not check an applicant's information as thoroughly as they perhaps should.

However, I would always strongly caution anyone against telling anything but the truth on their CV. You can easily become unstuck during an interview as a result.

STATISTIC

Surveys show that approximately 30 per cent of candidates 'lie' to one degree or another at interview.

For a longer discussion on this topic please refer back to Chapter 18, 'Basic principles'.

13 Being critical of others

Having problems with the boss is the top reason people give (in surveys) for changing jobs. However, you should never say anything negative about either a current or a previous employer.

Criticising your current employer is considered one of the top mistakes you can make at interview and will most likely cost you the job regardless of whether or not your criticism is justified.

BLOOPER!

Having delivered a particularly devastating critique of their current employer, one candidate was rather shocked to discover that their current employer was in fact the interviewer's brother-in-law!

Likewise, you should avoid criticising current or former colleagues.

There are a number of different interview questions you need to look out for on this front:

Question 3 in Chapter 19, 'The top 10 interview questions'.
Questions 14, 26 and 27 in Chapter 20, 'Fifty more classic questions: be prepared'.
Questions 5 and 10 in Chapter 21, 'The top 25 tough questions: taking the heat'.

14 Failing to ask your own questions

Interviews are always a two-way process. Not preparing your own questions for the end of an interview is therefore a common – and significant – interview mistake.

There aren't many interviews that conclude without the candidate being asked, 'Do you have any questions for me/us?' Almost all interviewers will give you a chance to ask questions and you should use this as an opportunity to further demonstrate your interest and enthusiasm. If you don't then you'll come across as passive and uninterested.

STATISTIC

A recent survey showed that 29 per cent of recruiters, when questioned, stated that the candidate not asking questions – or asking poor questions – at the end of the interview was sufficient reason for them to 'fail' them.

What should you ask when it's time for you to ask your own questions?

Please see Chapter 25, 'Ending the interview: your own questions'.

15 Prematurely talking money

It's best to avoid asking questions about pay and holidays – unless of course the interviewer brings up these topics themself. Such matters can always be covered in later discussions. Bringing them up during your interview can place too much focus on what you are expecting from the employer – rather than what you are offering them. This is never a good idea.

Topics to avoid talking about are covered in Chapter 25, 'Ending the interview: your own questions'.

And if you'd like advice on how to handle the interviewer asking you questions about pay, then take a look at Questions 47 and 48 in Chapter 20, 'Fifty more classic questions: be prepared'.

16 Not following up after the interview

Yes, I know I said this chapter would cover the 15 commonest interview mistakes – but everyone loves a bonus, don't they!

So here's a sixteenth mistake for you: not following up after the interview.

And that will be the subject of the next chapter.

PART 5

AFTER THE INTERVIEW: CLOSING THE DEAL

Chapter 27

Following up

So you have been to the interview and you think it went well. You should hear one way or the other within a week or so of the interview taking place, unless the interviewer specified otherwise.

But that doesn't mean you should just sit and wait – which is precisely what 90 per cent of people do.

At no stage in your job hunt should you be sitting back and waiting for anything – not until you've achieved the ultimate goal of successfully receiving a job offer. In a tight job market you need to be proactive and constantly keep up your efforts to land a new job.

You need to have a follow-up strategy in place.

What is a follow-up strategy?

The first thing to do – immediately after the interview – is to write (by post or by email) a brief letter, ostensibly to thank the interviewer for their time but actually to seize one last opportunity to make an impact. You want to reiterate how your skills and experience do of course meet their requirements.

So few people take the time to do this that you will stand out in the interviewer's mind – at the very moment when they will be making a crucial decision concerning your future.

It won't guarantee you the job but it can only help.

Is it really worth the effort?

Once you've got to the interview stage, the odds are already narrowing down very much in your favour. There could easily have been as many as 100 initial applicants. However, fewer than ten are likely to have been invited for interview. Success is within your grasp and one final effort at this stage can really swing things in your favour.

TOP TIP

You probably devoted a good hour or two of your time just to attending the interview and yet it doesn't take more than 15 minutes to knock out a well-crafted thank-you letter.

How do I go about this?

Follow up as soon as you can after the interview, either the same day if possible or, at the latest, the next day. By the time a recruiter has reached the interview stage, decisions can be made very quickly. You need to get your final shot in there before it's too late.

If the person whom you originally contacted is not the same as the person who interviewed you then you should send the letter to the person who actually interviewed you. If you were interviewed by more than one person then send it to whichever one of them arranged the interview with you (or with the recruitment agency representing you).

> *I am writing to thank you for taking the time to interview me on 10 June and to confirm my strong interest in the Sales Manager vacancy. I would also like to reiterate the qualities which I believe make me ideally suited to the role:*

You can follow this introduction with a few key sales points – and it is perfectly acceptable to use bullet points and put these points across in list form.

You can conclude your letter along the lines of:

> *I look forward to hearing from you once a decision has been reached. In the meantime, please do not hesitate to call me on 07700 900 159 should you require any further information.*

This is a fairly straightforward example and you can of course expand on it if appropriate. You may have thought of an important point since the interview which might further support your case. You may be able to refer to something that the interviewer mentioned that was of particular interest. There are numerous possibilities, but don't go over the top; at the end of the day it's only really a thank-you letter.

Brilliant Cover Letters

If you would like to learn more about such letters then please take a look at my comprehensive book on the subject, *Brilliant Cover Letters.* You can place your order for a copy via the following page on our website:

WEB LINK http://www.ineedacv.co.uk/brilliantcoverletters

Sometimes you just have to pick up the phone

If a week passes after sending this letter and you still haven't heard anything, then don't be shy to telephone the organisation and enquire politely whether a decision has been reached.

Unfortunately, not all organisations will bother to notify candidates of a negative decision.

Keeping track of your job hunt

We've put together a spreadsheet for you to help you keep track of the interviews you attend – who with, what date, etc. Not only that, but it'll let you keep track of the CVs you have sent out as well.

This tracking tool will help you to know exactly whether and when to follow up on an application and, quite simply, it will prevent you from becoming very confused! Much better to keep yourself organised – and this Excel spreadsheet will enable you to do just that.

To download your free copy, please visit the following link:

WEB LINK http://www.ineedacv.co.uk/tracker

Chapter **28**

Negotiating the offer

Congratulations! You've got a job offer on the table!

Whilst, in many cases, an employer might make a straightforward offer and you will be inclined to accept it without question, there will be occasions when you may wish to negotiate the precise details of their offer. If you're unprepared, this can be a difficult stage to handle. However, as always, if you've done your research and thought the matter through, your end goal is now very much in sight.

The package

There's a reason this chapter is called, 'Negotiating the offer' and not, 'Negotiating your salary'. It's because, depending on your circumstances, there could be a whole hoard of other factors you need to take into account besides just your salary:

- Cash: bonuses; profit-share; commission; overtime; staff discounts.
- Time: holiday allowance; time off in lieu.
- Sickness: sick pay.
- Car: company car; car allowance; car insurance.
- Training: training opportunities; training allowance.
- Medical benefits: private health insurance; dental plan; health club membership.
- Pension: pension plans; pension contributions.
- Childcare.
- Share options.
- Termination: notice period; 'gardening leave'; non-compete clauses.

In most cases, salary will be the most important item on your list – and will be the main focus of this chapter – but you mustn't lose sight of other factors which constitute the total package. Depending on the nature of these 'extras', they could make a relatively low basic salary seem much more attractive.

You should also take into account the effect this job is going to have on your CV. If it's going to help you develop in ways that will be of significant value to you in your next job (and will consequently boost your next salary package) then you may be prepared to accept a lower offer in order to secure the job – maybe even lower than what you are currently earning.

Market research

The very first step you should take (and should have taken long before a formal offer comes your way) is to research the kind of package usually offered for the type of position for which you are applying. To put it another way, you need to establish your market value. It is vital for you to have a realistic idea of what you should be worth to the employer – and it's vital for you to have this before you even start looking for jobs.

If you're working with a recruitment consultant, they can normally help you with this. However, there is plenty of information to be gleaned through looking at other job adverts and by checking online.

Once you've established a range for your market value, you need to decide:

- What is the minimum that you would be prepared to accept, assuming the job is suitably attractive?
- What is the maximum you can reasonably expect to achieve without breaking the deal?

Only you can decide what the minimum is that you would be prepared to accept, but your research should make it clear what the maximum is that you are likely to achieve.

The salary question

We've already established in a previous chapter that 'What is your current salary package?' and 'What salary package are you expecting for this role?' are popular interview questions.

While your current salary is a matter of fact, my advice for handling the second question was to dodge it slightly and quote a range of possibilities rather than give a precise answer. It's always best to wait until a firm job offer is being made before going into detail on this issue.

That time has now come.

While you will now need to be specific as to your requirements, it remains important (with a few exceptions, e.g. sales and other money-driven and largely commission-based roles) to convey the impression that money is not the only deciding factor in your choice of a new job and a new employer. Instead, your emphasis should be on politely but firmly conveying that you are aware of your value and that you feel it is only appropriate that you should be remunerated accordingly.

If your prospective employer makes the first move

In most cases your prospective employer will make the first move and tell you what they are prepared to offer. This has both advantages and disadvantages. The main advantage is that the company has shown its hand and you now know how close to (or far from) your own expectations their expectations are. The main disadvantage is that if the offer isn't sufficient then the onus is on you to make the next move.

If you are expected to make the first move

If an employer makes no specific offer but asks you to name your price, then they're certainly on the spot.

Your approach should be to try to identify whether or not they at least have a salary range in mind. An employer will normally have established such a range but, if challenged to reveal it, will probably err on the side of caution – so don't be immediately disappointed if your salary requirements exceed the range quoted.

The next move

Regardless of how the negotiations kick off, you should be aiming to pitch for a salary at the top end of the range – and consequently be prepared to negotiate and reduce that figure as necessary in order to reach a compromise. This is a standard haggling technique. Start high and be prepared to come down.

Bargaining strategies

The most important bargaining strategy at your disposal is to play this employer off against others. Politely point out that you have applications in progress for other roles where the packages offered are more in line with your requirements – and that you would naturally expect this employer to be able to at least match these offers, if not improve upon them. Whether or not you have firm offers from anyone else is, to a degree, beside the point; the point is to reiterate your market value to the employer – and to establish that you, entirely reasonably, expect to receive what you're worth.

If you're unable to adopt this strategy, then your next best strategy is to come clean and state the market research you have undertaken, give the employer the salary range you have identified and then make your case as to why you feel the high end of that scale best reflects your worth. If you've reached this stage then you've clearly already made a strong case at interview – and the employer now wants you. This is to your advantage. However, you may still need to make a final pitch to secure the level of salary you desire.

Reaching agreement

Once you've both got your cards on the table, a discussion may follow – and it may take compromises on both your parts in order to finally reach agreement.

There are so many different ways in which this conversation may unfold that it's impossible for me to provide you with a precise winning formula. For a start, you may be negotiating in person, via a recruitment consultant, by telephone or even in writing.

TOP TIP

Whatever happens, keep your cool and maintain a professional detachment. Don't let the discussions become at all heated, and demonstrate to the employer that you are willing to work with them to reach a mutually beneficial agreement. The confident manner in which you handle the negotiations may be sufficient grounds alone for the employer to feel you warrant more than their original offer.

The worst-case scenario

There's normally nothing to be lost in attempting to negotiate a higher salary than the employer originally offers. Provided you handle the proceedings in a diplomatic fashion, the worst possible outcome is likely to be that the employer sticks to their guns and refuses to contemplate a higher offer. However, having come this far (recruiting is an expensive process), most employers will usually display at least a little flexibility. If they do refuse to budge then it's up to you to decide whether or not their offer is sufficient or whether you will have to reject it. Be warned that, if you do flatly reject the offer, the chances of it being increased at this stage will not be high.

Another possible downside to negotiating is that, feeling they have initially paid 'over the odds' for you, employers might be rather ungenerous when it comes to reviewing your salary in the future. However, a bird in the hand is definitely worth two in the bush and, if an employer fails to give you the pay rises you deserve, you can always look elsewhere.

Considering the offer

Once the employer has made their final offer, you are under no obligation to accept it on the spot. It's entirely acceptable – and definitely recommended – to at least sleep on it. Such a major decision requires careful consideration and most employers will respect you for taking a little time to think it over.

Multiple and counter-offers

Another reason for taking at least 24 hours to consider an offer is that it will give you a chance to use this offer to influence others you may have received. If you've worked hard on your job hunt then it's not unusual to get to a position where you are confronted with multiple offers. While there are obvious risks involved, you can attempt to play them off against each other so as to achieve an even stronger offer.

Bear in mind that it's not just prospective employers who might make you a counter-offer. Your own current employer might well do so. But we'll cover that later in Chapter 30, 'Resigning'.

Get it in writing

Once you have reached final agreement, it is absolutely essential to get the offer in writing. This should confirm the precise details of the package being offered. It is vital to have this in hand before you contemplate resigning from your current position. I can't stress enough how important this is. A verbal offer can be withdrawn at any time and you could find yourself in a very difficult position.

It is worth noting that, in the UK, there is no legal requirement for a written contract of employment. A contract is deemed to exist the moment you accept a job offer. However, an employer is still required to give you (normally within two months of your start date) what is known as a 'written statement of employment particulars' detailing certain key terms of your employment.

Whilst a written offer on the employer's part is normally legally binding, it is common practice for it to be subject to suitable references. And that is the subject of the next chapter.

Chapter 29

References

Most offers of employment will be subject to your prospective employer being able to obtain satisfactory references. Indeed, some employers will withhold making an offer of employment until they have finished obtaining references.

Of course, not all employers will bother with this formality. With people being increasingly worried, for legal reasons, about giving anyone a bad reference, the whole references game can often seem a fairly pointless exercise. And it has, of course, been known for an individual's current employer to give a glowing reference just because they are keen for them to leave!

Nevertheless, many employers will still pursue references and, in certain lines of work, they can take the issue of references very seriously indeed.

Who to choose?

Naturally, you need to choose carefully! Their comments could have a significant impact on your application.

Traditionally, you are expected to be able to provide details of at least two referees – usually one 'personal' (often a former teacher or lecturer) and one 'professional' (usually your current or previous employer). However, it is not unheard of for an employer to want to check not only with your current employer but also with your previous employer and maybe even your employer before that. It all depends on how thorough they want to be – and how sensitive a role it is that you are being recruited for.

How to proceed?

While you could just dish out name and contact details on request, it is much better etiquette to actually contact your potential referees before releasing their details. Normally you won't have to worry about this until the interview stage but some employers will insist on having details of referees up front – as will some recruitment agencies.

Generally, it doesn't hurt to start getting in touch with potential referees early. This also gives them a chance to prepare what they will say about you – and gives you a chance to decide if they really are the best choice.

TOP TIP

Details of referees generally shouldn't be included on your CV. They're a waste of valuable space! They clutter it up and, more importantly, you will find that your referees get pestered unnecessarily by time wasters. By the time they have handled their umpteenth enquiry of the day, they are a lot less likely to say nice things about you! A simple sentence saying that they are available upon request is sufficient.

Depending on your relationship with your referee, you may find it is quickest and easiest to just pick up the phone. However, in most cases a brief but courteous letter will be appreciated.

Very occasionally you may be expected to secure a formal written reference yourself but in the vast majority of cases all you need to do is obtain permission to release your referees' contact details to any interested parties. It's then up to your prospective employer to decide how they wish to proceed.

Chapter 30

Resigning

There are, of course, various different ways of approaching the resignation process: some right and some wrong. You might be leaving your current employer but it never hurts to leave them with a positive impression of you.

There are only two points you really have to get across when resigning:

- The fact that you're resigning.
- Your acceptance that you are (probably) bound by a notice period.

Anything else is just a nicety.

But it's well worth being as nice as possible about the matter.

Harsh words in a letter of resignation could easily come back to haunt you in the future – not least if you ever need a reference from this employer.

Why are you leaving?

Your employer is, of course, going to be wondering why you're leaving. The important thing is to realise that you're under no obligation to go into any details. In fact, you're under no obligation to give any reason at all. You could simply say that you've decided the time is right to 'move on to a new challenge'. While they might be curious to know more, discretion will prevent many employers from prying any further.

Don't burn your bridges

Make the effort to thank your employer for the opportunity they have given you and wish them the best for the future. Keep it very simple and businesslike – whilst at the same time avoiding being cold and distant. There is nothing to be gained by burning bridges. You certainly shouldn't make any derogatory or disparaging comments about the organisation – or any other employee of the organisation.

You may find it hard to resist voicing particular concerns. However, whether or not your comments are justified, using your letter of resignation to launch a personal attack or to attempt to score points is highly ill-advised. Your intention may simply be to make your employer aware of a particular problem but such a letter can nonetheless end up sounding vindictive – and is unlikely to ever do you any good.

Notice periods

In most jobs you will be bound by a period of notice, stipulated in your contract of employment. You should study your contract carefully so as to be aware of precisely what this period of notice is.

You should also identify how many leave days you remain entitled to – since these could reduce your notice period.

While you are not under any legal obligation to give more than this statutory period of notice, in certain circumstances you may wish to do so. If this is the case then this should be made clear in your letter – with a statement indicating precisely when it is you wish to leave.

Don't delay!

Resignation letters should generally be sent as soon as possible after you have reached a firm decision to leave. Your decision only becomes legally binding on delivery of your letter of resignation. It should be noted that you don't need to post your letter; email is also legally binding.

Exit interviews

Upon receipt of an employee's resignation, many employers will wish to conduct what is known as an 'exit interview'. During such an interview, they may try to probe your reasons for leaving in greater detail, ostensibly to identify improvements they might be able to make to the working environment or to specific practices and procedures.

TOP TIP

As with your original letter, keep your comments at an exit interview professional, not personal. Remember that an employer can't force you to disclose your reasons. Don't let yourself be talked into a corner. While you may have kept your cool in your letter, it can be harder to do so face to face.

Counter-offers

Your employer may try to encourage you to stay with them, so you need to be prepared to face the possibility that you may be offered an improvement to the salary package you currently receive.

You might well be very tempted to accept such an offer, so it is important to remember your specific reasons for wanting to resign in the first place. Was money really your main motivator?

You may even be offered a promotion or a move to a different branch or department. This sort of counter-offer will take more serious thought on your part. How does the new job you've been offered compare with the one you are planning to go to?

While I'm not saying you shouldn't give serious consideration to counter-offers – and in some cases accept them – I would say that you should proceed with caution.

Rejecting other offers

Besides resigning from your current position, it is also very important to write to politely decline any other job offers you may have received.

This is more than a common courtesy; it is yet another step in building a strong reputation for yourself as a serious and professional individual.

Clearly the organisation you're turning down has invested a lot of time and effort in dealing with you. It's going to expect some sort of reason from you for rejecting the offer – and you're going to have to give one.

You might have felt your prospective future line manager was cold and distant when you met at interview. You might have felt the salary offer was a joke. You might feel that your future career prospects would be limited within this particular organisation. But is it really going to be to your advantage to tell them any of that? It might make you feel better but it isn't going to do anything to increase your standing in their eyes. You should always be very careful of projecting any negative emotion into a letter.

You should always bear in mind that you might end up dealing with this same organisation again at some stage. If they have made you an offer, then they obviously have a positive impression of you – and you want them to maintain that.

Chapter **31**

Handling rejection

It is a sad fact of life that, no matter how capable, qualified and experienced you are, most interviews will result in rejection for one reason or another. So you had better get used to it! Nearly everybody suffers a few such setbacks when they are hunting for a new job; many job hunters are regularly shot down in flames. Remember: it just wasn't your destiny.

If you were not successful, try to treat the interview as a learning experience. A real, live interview is the very best form of interview practice you can get! We all make mistakes; make sure that you use them to your advantage for your next interview.

Naturally, if you had your heart set on a particular opportunity and have been through the highs and lows of being invited to a first interview and then to a second – or maybe even an assessment centre – then it can be very demoralising to find out, that at the end of the day, the job went to someone else and all your efforts were for nothing.

Or were they ...

Never say never

Your initial reaction to receiving a rejection from a prospective employer might be, if you're a philosophical sort of person, to conclude that it's the end of this particular road and that you need to turn your attentions to other possibilities you've got on the go.

However, call me stubborn, but I – and many other recruitment professionals – still recommend following up on such a rejection with a brief but important letter.

Allow me to explain why:

- You have quite probably worked pretty hard to get to this stage.
- They don't want to hire you now but may well be interested in the future.
- It should only take you five minutes to fire off this letter.

Building bridges

Having taken the time to build bridges with this organisation, you'd be as well to maintain those bridges as best you can. You never know when your contacts might come in handy later in your career.

- You might end up getting a job where you deal on a regular basis with this organisation.
- You may have missed out on the current vacancy but there could be another one in just a few weeks' time.
- What if the person who won the job subsequently turns it down?

TOP TIP

Having invested this much in your relationship, it makes sense to seize the opportunity to spend a few more minutes developing that relationship even further.

Maintaining a positive attitude

The way you approach writing this letter is, of course, very important. You might feel a degree of resentment for them, having made you jump through lots of hoops only to ultimately disappoint you – but you certainly don't want that kind of negative emotion to come through in your letter.

There isn't (or at least there shouldn't be) anything personal about the decision: 'It's just business.' You are not being rejected as an individual; your candidature for this particular vacancy is being rejected. In many cases it could be an extremely arbitrary decision; if you're faced with a number of high-quality candidates then it can be very hard to choose between them. Indeed, sometimes there is so little to choose between candidates that, more than anything, success or failure is down to luck.

It is, of course, fine to express your disappointment but you should definitely avoid sounding bitter! A negative attitude is unlikely to make a good impression.

You should instead attempt to extract some constructive feedback from them so as to help you with future applications you make. Most recruiters won't volunteer this information; you'll have to ask for it. You might just get back the usual canned response that 'it was an extremely difficult decision', etc., etc. You might get no reply whatsoever. But you might just get some really useful advice, which could enable you to address any weaknesses or rectify any mistakes so that you have a greater chance of success the next time around.

Down but not out

You're also demonstrating that you're somebody who doesn't like to lose and who will do their utmost to make sure they're less likely to lose out again in the future.

Remember: there is a job out there with your name on it and, if no one has yet recognised your star quality, it's up to you to dazzle them!

Of course, if you're having difficulty getting yourself invited to interview in the first place then it may very well be that your CV needs some work.

The CV Book

If you would like to learn more about CV writing, then please take a look at my comprehensive book on the subject, *The CV Book*. You can place your order for a copy via the following page on our website:

WEB LINK http://www.ineedacv.co.uk/thecvbook

Summary

- Immediately after the interview write to thank the interviewer for their time – and seize the opportunity to make a further impact on them.
- A verbal offer can be withdrawn at any time, so it is absolutely essential to get the offer in writing.
- When resigning, it never hurts to leave your employer with a positive impression of you. It's well worth being as nice as possible about the matter.
- If you were not successful, try to treat the interview as a learning experience. We all make mistakes; make sure you use them to your advantage for your next interview.
- Remember: there is a job out there with your name on it and, if no one has yet recognised your star quality, it's up to you to dazzle them!

PART 6

MY FIVE TOP TIPS FOR INTERVIEW SUCCESS

Chapter 32

Interview success

If you only had time to read two pages of *The Interview Book*, these are the pages I would most like you to have taken the time to read. See it as a 'cheat sheet'. It encapsulates the most important principles that we have covered in the book. Make an effort to accommodate all these for your interview and you'll immediately be well above average.

1 Be prepared

The key to preventing pre-interview jitters is preparation. If you are to be able to convince a recruiter that you are right for the role then you obviously first need to get it clear in your own mind why you are right for the role. As well as researching the job itself, you should also research the organisation.

2 Make sure you're there on time

Yes, it may seem so obvious, yet late arrival is consistently one of the very top reasons cited by recruiters for their rejecting candidates at interview stage. Don't be late. Better than that, aim to get there early so as to have time to relax and compose yourself.

3 Create answers to potential questions

It's essential for you to think for yourself and create your own answers to potential questions. Wherever possible, try to integrate real-life examples into your answers rather than just speaking hypothetically. Flagging up specific, relevant examples from your own experience is an ideal way of reinforcing your points in the interviewer's mind.

4 Don't recite your answers parrot-fashion

Too many candidates make the mistake of sounding like they're reciting answers from an interview book. Even if you have prepared and memorised your own answers, you should be careful to make sure that your delivery is natural and doesn't come across as rehearsed.

5 Be confident and show your enthusiasm

Confident people inspire confidence in others – if you appear confident that you are able to do the job, the employer is likely to be more inclined to believe that you can – and showing a lack of enthusiasm is generally fatal to your chances of success. Be enthusiastic – and show it. Confidence and enthusiasm are traits that are guaranteed to impress an interviewer.

Conclusion

Successfully passing an interview is not rocket science! Most of what I have outlined is reasonably simple to take on board and it's just a matter of putting in the necessary time and effort.

I do hope you have found *The Interview Book* useful. Don't forget to visit The CV Centre's online forum to let us know how you get on.

WEB LINK http://www.ineedacv.co.uk/forum

You will also have the opportunity to make contact with me and my team directly.

GOOD LUCK!

Further reading and resources

Recommended books

Borg, J. (2007) *Persuasion: The Art of Influencing People*, Harlow: Prentice Hall Business.

Borg, J. (2008) *Body Language: 7 Easy Lessons to Master the Silent Language*, Harlow: Prentice Hall Life.

Bright, J. and Earl, J. (2008) *Brilliant CV*, 3rd edition, Harlow: Prentice Hall Business.

Edenborough, R. (2009) *Brilliant Psychometric Tests*, Harlow: Prentice Hall Business.

Fagan, A. (2007) *Brilliant Job Hunting*, 2nd edition, Harlow: Prentice Hall Business.

Faust, B. and Faust, M. (2006) *Pitch Yourself*, 2nd edition, Harlow: Prentice Hall Business.

Hall, R. (2008) *The Secrets of Success at Work: 10 Steps to Accelerating Your Career*, Harlow: Prentice Hall Business.

Hodgson, S. (2007) *Brilliant Tactics to Pass Aptitude Tests*, 2nd edition, Harlow: Prentice Hall Business.

Hodgson, S. (2008) *Brilliant Answers to Tough Interview Questions*, 3rd edition, Harlow: Prentice Hall Business.

Innes, J. (2009) *Brilliant Cover Letters*, Harlow: Prentice Hall Business.

Innes, J. (2009) *The CV Book*, Harlow: Prentice Hall Business.

Jay, R. (2008) *Brilliant Interview*, 2nd edition, Harlow: Prentice Hall Business.

Perkins, G. (2007) *Killer CVs & Hidden Approaches*, 3rd edition, Harlow: Prentice Hall Business.

Templar, R. (2002) *The Rules of Work: A Definitive Guide to Personal Success*, Harlow: Prentice Hall Business.

Yeung, R. (2008) *Confidence: The Art of Getting Whatever You Want*, Harlow: Prentice Hall Life.

These titles are available from all major bookshops. You can also learn more about them and even place an order for a copy by visiting the following page on our website:

WEB LINK http://www.ineedacv.co.uk/recommendedbooks2

Online resources

I keep my list of online resources – online. That way I can keep it bang up to date at all times. Please access the following page for a wide range of useful links to job sites and other online resources.

WEB LINK http://www.ineedacv.co.uk/resources

Index

Also from **JAMES INNES**

Founder of The CV Centre, the UK's leading CV consultancy

Your CV has less than 30 seconds to win you an interview and it needs to be exceptional.

The CV Book reveals all the tips and tricks you need to ensure your CV ends up on the 'yes' pile.

9780273721741

Find out: Exactly what you need to say and how to say it • How to build a CV • The 15 most common mistakes and how to avoid them • Five easy ways to make your CV really shine • And much more...

9780273724636

Your cover letter is the first thing a recruiter will see.

It can make all the difference between success and failure so you need to get it right.

Brilliant Cover Letters is packed with invaluable advice that is tried, tested and proven on a daily basis.

Includes:

• Online templates available for free download and immediate use • Suitable templates for all purposes, from graduates to executives • Specific templates for jobs such as legal, medical, IT, teaching • and much more ...

No matter what your age, background, job or level of experience, these books will help you become the perfect candidate.

Prentice Hall is an imprint of